Understanding Science 1

Understanding Science 1

Joe Boyd

Head of Chemistry, Beeslack High School, Penicuik

and

Walter Whitelaw

Assistant Science Adviser, Lothian

JOHN MURRAY

Advisory panel
Peter Leckstein: Head of Science, Burntwood School
Lesley Campbell: ILEA Health Education Adviser
Terry Allsop: Lecturer in Education Studies, Oxford University

First published 1989
by John Murray (Publishers) Ltd.
50 Albemarle Street, London W1X 4BD

Reprinted 1989

Designed by Impress International, Manchester
Typeset by Wilmaset, Birkenhead
Printed by Cayfosa Industria Grafica, Spain

British Library Cataloguing in Publication Data
Boyd, Joe
  Understanding science 1.
  1. Science – For schools
  I. Title   II. Whitelaw, Walter
  500

  ISBN 0–7195–4621–4 Pupils' book
  ISBN 0–7195–4622–2 Teachers' resource book

Contents

Extensions

Introduction

A   How to use this book

1.1 First experiments

Always write your titles in your book.

A   Mixing chemicals

Science is all about finding ways to understand the world around you. Learning to look closely is your first step to becoming a scientist.

Read all the information.

Looking closely

Not looking closely

Look closely at what happens during this experiment.
Remember to read the whole page before you begin.

Collect what you need.

Collect

Test-tube rack
Test tube
2 bottles of
different chemicals
Safety glasses

1 Add a
little of
one
chemical
to the test
tube.

2 Add a little of
the other
chemical to
the test tube.
Look closely.

3 Clean the test
tube.
Return the
bottles of
chemicals.

Carry out the instructions. Remember to read all the instructions first.

4 Answer the questions below.
5 Follow the instructions again with two different chemicals.

Answer the questions in complete sentences.

1 What is the name of the first chemical? What colour is it?
2 What is the name of the second chemical? What colour is it?

3 What happened
when the chemicals
were mixed? The
following words
might help you.

CLOUDY   LUMPY
CLEAR
FIZZY   COLOUR CHANGES
NOTHING
HAPPENS

Have your work checked by your teacher, who will tell you what to do next.

B Following instructions

It is important to read and then to follow instructions carefully in science. Sometimes there are a lot of instructions. These need to be done in the right order to make your experiment work.

Collect

Piece of white paper

1 Write down the time on the upper left-hand corner of the paper.

2 Fold the paper **carefully** in half.

3 Fold the paper again into quarters.

4 Unfold the paper. Write the letters *I* and *A* in the upper left-hand quarter of the page. Use **large** letters and write in your **best** handwriting.

5 Find something in your bag to cover up the letters.

6 Write the letters *D*, *O* and *N* in the bottom left-hand quarter of the paper. Hide these letters with something. Your paper should now look like this.

7 Write the letters *M* and *A* in the top right-hand quarter of the paper.

8 Write the letters *K*, *E* and *Y* in the bottom right-hand quarter of the paper.

9 Remove everything from the paper.

10 Draw a line between the *I* and the first *A*. Draw another line between the *M* and the second *A*.

11 Put your hands on top of your head. Read the hidden message. Say hee-haw, hee-haw!

12 Do not follow instructions 4 to 11.

13 Write the time in the bottom right-hand corner of the paper.

1

This is science

A Mixing chemicals

Science is all about finding ways to understand the world around you. Learning to look closely is your first step to becoming a scientist.

Looking closely

Not looking closely

Look closely at what happens during this experiment.
Remember to read the whole page before you begin.

Collect

Test-tube rack
Test tube
2 bottles of
different chemicals
Safety glasses

1 Add a little of one chemical to the test tube.

2 Add a little of the other chemical to the test tube. Look closely.

3 Clean the test tube.
Return the bottles of chemicals.

4 Answer the questions below.
5 Follow the instructions again with two different chemicals.

1 What is the name of the first chemical? What colour is it?
2 What is the name of the second chemical? What colour is it?

3 What happened when the chemicals were mixed? The following words might help you.

CLOUDY
CLEAR LUMPY
FIZZY
COLOUR CHANGES
NOTHING HAPPENS

CHECKPOINT

B Seeing is believing

The photographs below are of everyday objects. They have been taken from an unusual angle. Look closely at the photograph for hints about the object.

Write down the name of each object.
What was the best hint in each photograph?

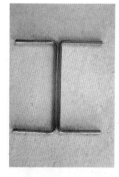    

Collect a copy of the drawings below and stick it into your book.

What **two** things can you see in each picture?

A   Junior reporter

A scientist follows instructions and looks closely at what is happening. The good scientist then writes a complete report. Your next step is to learn this skill. You will start by writing very simple reports.

Writing carefully

I mixed clear sodium carbonate with blue copper sulphate. The result was a cloudy blue mixture.

Good! This work is tidy and accurate

Writing carelessly

Sodium Cabinate waz invisible if went blue fuzzy the other wos sulfate

Copy the spelling from the bottle. Try to write neatly

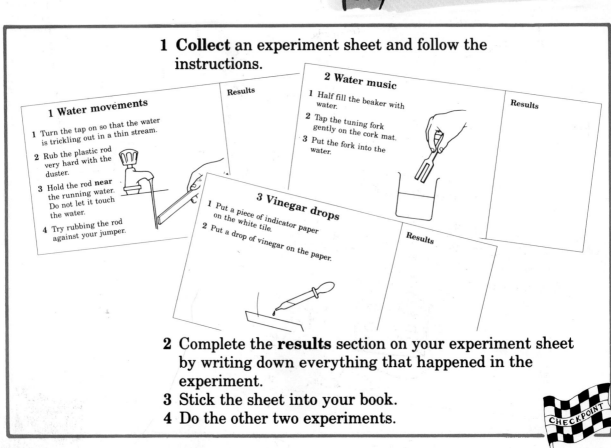

1 Collect an experiment sheet and follow the instructions.

1 Water movements

1 Turn the tap on so that the water is trickling out in a thin stream.

2 Rub the plastic rod very hard with the duster.

3 Hold the rod **near** the running water. Do not let it touch the water.

4 Try rubbing the rod against your jumper.

Results

2 Water music

1 Half fill the beaker with water.

2 Tap the tuning fork gently on the cork mat.

3 Put the fork into the water.

Results

3 Vinegar drops

1 Put a piece of indicator paper on the white tile.

2 Put a drop of vinegar on the paper.

Results

2 Complete the **results** section on your experiment sheet by writing down everything that happened in the experiment.

3 Stick the sheet into your book.

4 Do the other two experiments.

CHECKPOINT

B Ace reporter

Practise your reporting skills by doing these three experiments. Report your results in the same way as before.

4 Watch the birdie

Results

1 Hold the knitting needle between your hands as shown.

2 Rub your hands together backwards and forwards. The needle will twirl.

3 Look at the picture card while you do this.

5 Fizzy veg

Results

1 Add a little clear liquid to a test tube.

2 Put a little chopped potato into the clear liquid.

3 Clean the test tube afterwards.

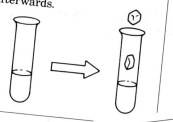

6 Seeing sound

Results

1 Look at the little screen.

2 Put your mouth close to the microphone and make a loud high noise. For example, whistle.

3 Make a low noise now.

A Safety rules

Sometimes you will do things in your experiments that could be dangerous. However, you will control these dangers. You will be safe.

For example, you can learn how to control

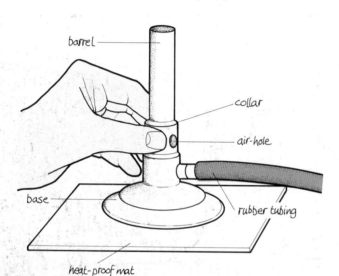

Your teacher will show you a **bunsen burner**. The bunsen burner will help you to control fire.

Collect

Bunsen burner
Heat-proof mat
Safety glasses
Coloured pencils

1 Put the bunsen burner on the heat-proof mat.
2 Close the air hole.
3 Push the rubber tube onto the gas tap.
4 Turn the gas tap on. Light the burner.
5 Open the air hole slowly. Watch the changes in the flame.

1 Make a large drawing of a bunsen burner.
   Colour the flame yellow.
   Label all the parts of your drawing.
2 Copy and complete the table below.

	Airhole		
	Closed	Half open	Open
Colour of flame			

3 The yellow flame is the safety flame.
   Why is it safer than other types of bunsen flame?

CHECKPOINT

B Classroom sense

1 Look at the cartoon below.
   Collect a copy and stick it into your book.
2 Put a red ring round each danger in the cartoon.
   Number each one. There are at least ten dangers.
3 Work with a partner. Make up and write down a safety
   rule to control five of the dangers in the cartoon.

Collect a list of safety rules. Keep them safe!

Design a sign

Your problem is to design labels for a shipment of dangerous chemicals. The chemicals are being delivered to a foreign country where nobody speaks English. There are three kinds of chemicals in the shipment:

- **Flammable**—these will catch fire easily
- **Poisonous**—these will kill
- **Explosive**—these could explode.

Collect

Design sheet
Coloured pencils

Here are some things to think about:
    Your label will have to go on a bottle.
    Should your label • be coloured?
                              • have words?
                              • be complicated?

Now solve the problem.

Draw your three labels on the design sheet and stick them in your book.

Ask your partner what he or she thinks of your labels. Ask him or her to write in the comment box on your sheet.

Life in 2020 AD

How do you think science and technology will have changed the world by the year 2020?

Alfred Nobel

Alfred Nobel was born in Sweden in 1833. He was a scientist and a businessman. In 1866 he invented dynamite and later on he discovered other explosives that were even more powerful. He then set up factories to make his explosives and became very rich indeed.

Alfred Nobel was worried that his inventions might be misused. He wanted to encourage people to work for the good of humanity. He decided to set up a fund to award prizes for the very best work in science, medicine, literature and peace. Nobel died in 1896 and the first Nobel Prizes were awarded in 1901.

Today most research scientists dream of the honour of receiving a Nobel Prize. Perhaps one of you will produce work that Alfred Nobel would have wanted to reward!

1 Copy and complete the personal history file about Alfred Nobel.

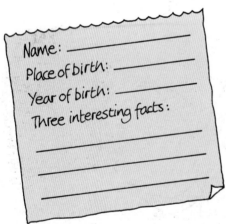

Name: —————

Place of birth: —————

Year of birth: —————

Three interesting facts:

—————

—————

—————

2 Use the books in the classroom or books from a library to find out more about Nobel and his work. Write a paragraph about what you find out. The key words to look up in the index are **Nobel, Nobel Prize, dynamite**.

Look alive

Set about sets

A Sorting

People often seem to make a room untidy. There are many objects around us and it is easy to get them in a muddle. For example, look at the science room below.

Describe four things that you would do to sort out the mess.

Collect

Box of objects

> Work with a partner.
> Sort the objects into **two** groups.
>
>

1 Copy and complete the table. Give each group a name. List the objects in each group.

First group: _ _ _ _ _ _	Second group: _ _ _ _ _ _

2 What did all the objects in the first group have in common?
3 What did all the objects in the second group have in common?
4 There are many different ways of sorting these objects into two groups. Write down as many ways as you can.
5 Why are there many right answers to this exercise?

CHECKPOINT

B Sets

This is an example of a set

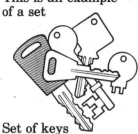

Set of keys

A **set** is a group of things which are similar. The things have something in common. They do not have to be **exactly** the same.

Sorting things into sets is very helpful. You can think about all the similar things together.

There are more than a million different kinds of animals on earth. We could sort them into sets like these.

Set of farm animals

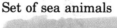

Set of sea animals

Collect

Tray of shapes

1 Sort the shapes into sets.
2 Describe your sets in your book.
   Make sure you write what each set has in common.

1 What is a set?
2 Why do we need to sort all the different animals into sets?
3 Look at these four sets of animals. Name each set. The first one has been done for you.

a *set of pets*   b   c   d

4 Why are there lots of possible names for each set?
5 Why is the cat in more than one set?

2.2 The set of living things

A What living things do

You belong to the most important set of things on the earth. You belong to the set of **living things**. Living things do what non-living things cannot do on their own.

Each cartoon hints at **one** thing which only living things can do. Look carefully at the cartoons. Discuss each one with your partner.

A DAY IN THE LIFE OF SQUEAKY the MOUSE.

1. My birth-day.

2. A breath of fresh air before lunch, then....

3. ....measure up for a new suit.

4. Greens for lunch. I won't leaf any!

5. Go across the road to visit my friend.

6. Help!

7. What a relief! Phew!

Copy and complete this table.

Cartoon	What the living thing is doing
1	
2	
3	
4	
5	
6	
7	

CHECKPOINT

B World zoo

You belong to the set of living things. Some other living things are shown below. They all belong to the same set, the set of living things.

coral
yeast
conifers
shark
liver fluke
moss
lizard
earwig
heron
bat
fly
earthworm
mouse
sea anemone
human
frog
sea-horse
mint
octopus
mould
barnacle

A set is a group of things which are similar. These living things must be similar in some way(s).

Collect
Pack of cards

1 Sort the cards into two sets. Set A must show living things. Set B must show non-living things.
2 Discuss the two sets of cards with a partner.

What is similar about **all** living things? Give at least five different answers.

A Examining a living thing

Copy

The best way to find out about living things is to study them with care. Animals and plants are alive. You should always treat them with care and respect.

Collect

Petri dish
Hand lens
Ruler

1 **Collect ONE** of the animals in a petri dish.
2 Follow the instructions on the opposite page. Answer the questions in sentences.

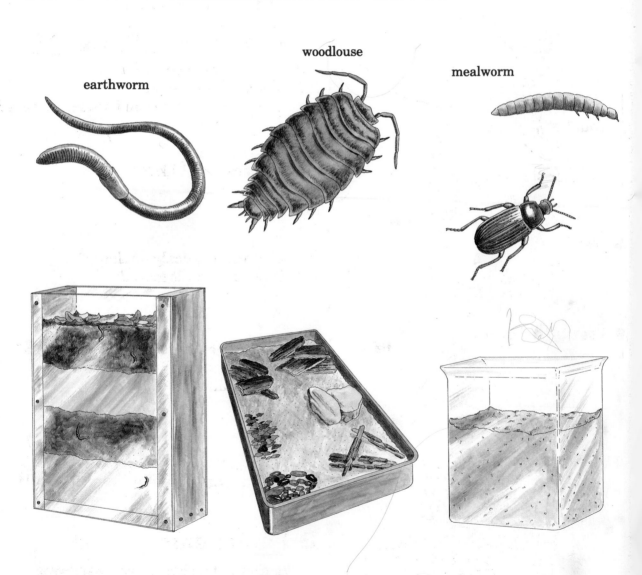

earthworm

woodlouse

mealworm

1 Name it.

What sort of animal is it?

2 Measure it.

a How long is the animal?
b How wide is the animal?

3 Examine it.

a What colour is the animal?
b Does it have

stripes   scales   rings

c How many legs does it have?
d Can you see any eyes?
e What else can you see on its head or body?

4 Touch it very gently.

a What does it do?
b What does it feel like?

5 Watch and listen.

a Does it move quickly or slowly?
b Is it noisy when it moves?

6 Look at its home.

a Describe where it lives.
b What evidence is there here that the animal is alive?

7 Draw the shape of the animal.

Label the parts that you know (e.g. legs, antennae, eyes).

B Look again

Ask your teacher for another living thing to examine.

A Be a good looker

A good scientist is always a good looker. She or he notices important details. You can begin to be a good scientist by looking carefully at objects and picking out the important details.

---

1 Copy these shapes.

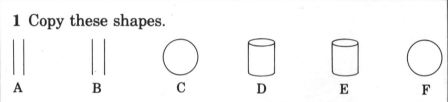

A   B   C   D   E   F

2 You will see six objects one after the other. You will see each object for 30 seconds.

3 Name each object.
Make the shape look like the object by adding no more than three important details to the shape.
For example, if you are shown a fish you could add a tail, a fin and an eye to the shape shown.

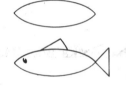

If you observe living things closely you see that some of them are similar. The similarities allow us to group living things into sets. These similarities are important details for a scientific observer.

The scientist puts animals into two main sets. The important detail is a **backbone**.

Animals with a backbone are called **vertebrates**.
Animals without a backbone are called **invertebrates**.

vertebrates   invertebrates

1 **a** What is the difference between the two sets of animals?
  b Why is it sometimes difficult to spot this important detail?
2 Look at the three sets below.
  a Which set contains four vertebrates?
  b Which sets contain four invertebrates?
  c Which animal is the odd one out in each set?

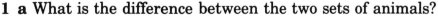

A

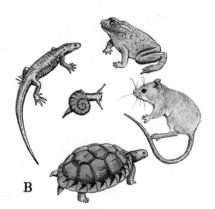

B

C

B A pupil's eye

You have been at your new school for many weeks now. How observant have you been? Answer these questions in **sentences.**

1 Where is the school boiler?
2 What colour is the headteacher's car or bike?
3 How many games fields are there in the grounds?
4 What colour is the floor inside the school office?
5 How many science teachers are there?
6 **Collect** a map of the school and some coloured pencils.
  Mark in the following important details:
    • colour the headteacher's office in red
    • colour the main car park in brown
    • colour the staffroom in yellow
    • colour any flower beds in green
    • Put a X beside the main entrance.
  Write what each colour means on your map and stick it into your book.
7 Copy this map of your teacher's face. **Without looking** colour in the correct eye colour and hair colour. Add three important details to improve the likeness.

An eye for the animals

A Observing an animal

Collect
An animal

You are now going to make scientific observations of one of the animals provided.

Remember, animals are living things and deserve to be treated with care and respect at all times. **Do not harm them**.

Care

Always complete the study of one animal before you go onto another.

Your observation will be in four parts.

1 Movement

2 Structure (What does it look like?)

3 Feeding

4 Habitat (Where does it live?)

The words on the opposite page will help you to spot and write about important details. **Write** a paragraph on each of the four parts of your observation. Always include a large **drawing** of the animal.

1 Movement

a *Type?* Fast, slow, still, jerky, smooth.
b *How?* Legs, fins, tail, wriggle, slide, glide, swim, jump, hop, run, scamper.
c *Reasons?* Eating, cleaning, being nosey, frightened, doing toilet, being friendly.

2 Structure

a *Size?* Big, small, mm, cm, estimate, breadth, length, height.
b *Shape?* Round, flat, thin, fat, head, tail.
c *Body covering?* Colour, skin, fur, scales, hair, wet, dry, soft, coarse.
d *Bits?* Legs, arms, wings, fins, number of, mouth, ears, eyes, antennae.

3 Feeding

a *What?* Plants, meat, alive, appearance, colour, amount, size.
b *How?* Teeth, claws, catch, jaws, chomp, chew, tear.

4 Habitat

a *Where?* Land, water, fresh, salty, air, under, over, build, scrape.
b *Conditions?* Dark, light, wet, dry, cold, hot.

B Keep watch

Make scientific observations of other animals. Your teacher will tell you when to stop.

2.6 Who is spineless?

A Sets of vertebrates

You should now be a good observer. This skill of looking closely at something to find the important details can help you to find better ways of putting animals into sets.

Collect

Pack of cards

Rules

- Play **Snap** in the usual way, but more quietly!
- If the top two cards on the pile are from the same vertebrate set then whisper 'Snap'.
- Use the five vertebrate sets: fish, birds, mammals, amphibians, reptiles.

1 Work with a partner. Shuffle the cards.
2 Sort the cards into these five different sets of **vertebrates**.

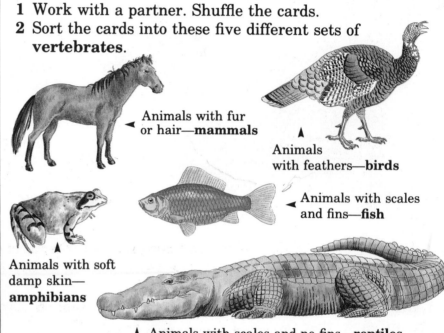

Animals with fur or hair—**mammals**

Animals with feathers—**birds**

Animals with scales and fins—**fish**

Animals with soft damp skin—**amphibians**

▲ Animals with scales and no fins—**reptiles**

3 Once you and your partner are sure of these sets, show them to your teacher. You must know these sets very well to be able to win the following game.
4 Now play the game (the rules are given on the left).

When you have finished copy and complete the table. Use your five card sets of vertebrates to help you.

Vertebrate group	Example	Body covering	Warm/ cold blooded	Eggs or live birth	Suckles young	Limbs
1. Mammals	Stoat	Furry/Hairy	Warm blooded			
2.						
3.						
4.						
5.						

B Using vertebrate sets

Look at these animals.

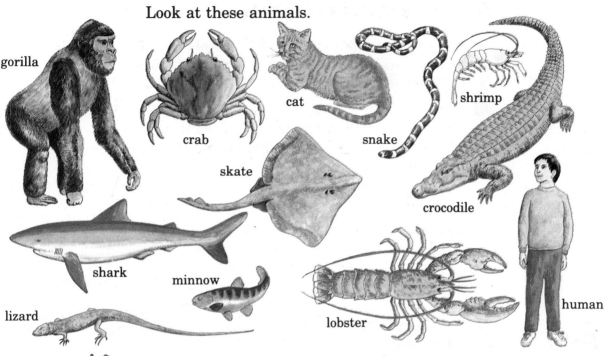

gorilla

crab

cat

snake

shrimp

skate

crocodile

shark

minnow

lobster

human

lizard

1 Divide the animals into four sets. Give each set a name and **write** the members of each set in your book.

2 A hawk and a penguin look very different. Yet both are members of the set of **birds**. This means that they are similar in some important details. **Write** down these important details.

hawk

penguin

Collect

Pack of cards

Happy Families
1 Deal all the cards out. (There should be at least three players.)
2 Try to collect a complete set—a **Happy Family**.
3 The player on the dealer's left begins by asking one of the other players for a card. She or he must name the set wanted and also identify the important detail on the card. For example, 'Please give me the mammal card with live birth'.
4 If the player gets the card then she or he has another turn. If not, then the next player has their turn.

CHECKPOINT

A Using keys

A scientist can identify an unknown object, such as a rock or an animal, by using a **key**. A key is easy to use. See if you can work this one out.

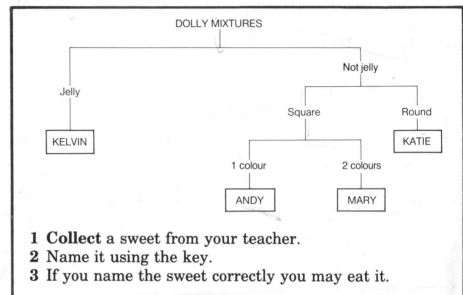

1 **Collect** a sweet from your teacher.
2 Name it using the key.
3 If you name the sweet correctly you may eat it.

1 Describe how you used the sweet key.
2 Use the key below to name these pond animals. Write the answers in your book.

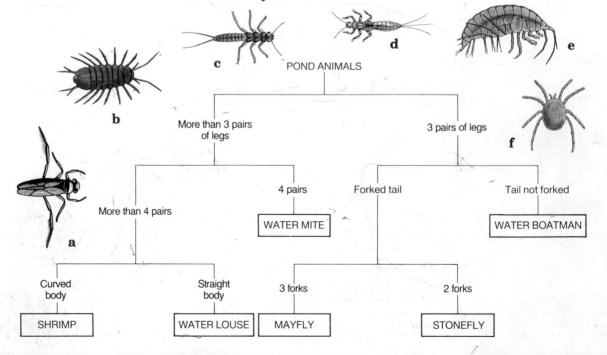

3 Use this key to name these crystals. Write the answers in your book.

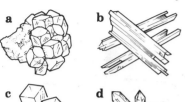

Key for crystals
1 Long needle-like crystals   Go to 2
  Block-like crystals   Go to 3
2 Pencil-like ends with six sides   **Quartz**
  Sliced ends with flat face   **Potassium nitrate**
3 Cube with sharp corners   **Common salt**
  Cube with sliced corners   **Galena**

B Key practice

1 Use the key to name these birds. Write the answers in your book.

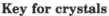

KNOW YOUR CROW

All black — Not all black

No baggy thighs — Baggy thighs → ROOK

White patches → MAGPIE — No white patches → JACKDAW

Rough throat → RAVEN — No rough throat → CARRION CROW

2 Use the key to name each scientist. Write the answers in your book.

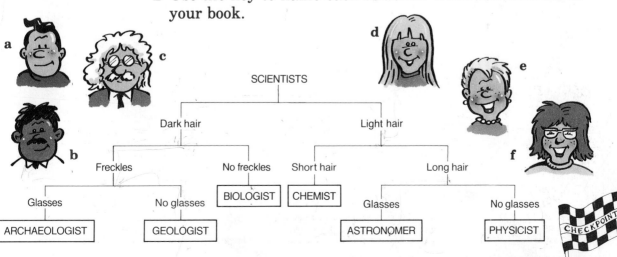

SCIENTISTS

Dark hair — Light hair

Freckles — No freckles → BIOLOGIST

Short hair → CHEMIST — Long hair

Glasses → ARCHAEOLOGIST — No glasses → GEOLOGIST

Glasses → ASTRONOMER — No glasses → PHYSICIST

CHECKPOINT

Problem

House a louse

Your problem is to help
Sneaky the woodlouse find a
pleasant home.

Collect

Dish with a
woodlouse in it
Empty dish
Filter papers
Beaker of water
Sandpaper
Black paper

Hints

- Does Sneaky like—rough or smooth ground?
  —damp or dry ground?
  —dark or light?

- You need to give Sneaky a choice in the dish.

- You need to record Sneaky's movements for a short
  time.

For example,

Sneaky's movements   Your record over the time

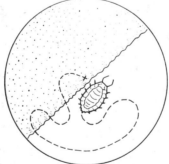

Now solve the problem.

Write a letter to the Housing Department. Tell them what
kind of house your friend Sneaky would prefer. They will
need some evidence so tell them about your experiments.

Talkabout

Life on other planets

Are there living things on other planets? What might they be like? How might we discover them?

Charles Darwin

Charles Darwin was born in 1809. He was the son of a doctor. When he was about your age, he collected things like postage franks (which are like stamps) and minerals.

In 1831 he volunteered to sail on a survey ship to South America. The voyage was to last five years, and it was the beginning of Charles Darwin's great work.

Whenever the ship stopped, Darwin went ashore in search of interesting animals and plants. He made studies of unusual living things and also of unusual rocks and crystals. He found some very strange animals living on the Galapagos Islands, for example iguanas, which are huge lizards. He also found fourteen different varieties of finches. Each kind had a different beak. Darwin was such a good scientist because he noticed details like this. He closely observed things. He then asked himself questions like:

- *Why are some animals so similar and yet they live on islands far away from each other?*
- *Why are some similar animals slightly different from each other?*
- *What causes the differences?*

Darwin sent samples back to Britain so that he could study them in more detail when he returned. He finally worked out how one kind of living thing could change slowly into another kind over a long period of time. This change is called evolution. Darwin wrote a famous book called 'On the origin of the species by means of natural selection' to explain his ideas. It was a best seller in 1859. Some of his ideas still cause arguments today.

Name: ——————
Place of birth: ——————
Year of birth: ——————
Three interesting facts:
——————
——————
——————
——————

1 Copy and complete the personal history file about Charles Darwin.

2 Use the books in the classroom or books from a library to find out more about Darwin and his work. Write a paragraph about what you find out. The key words to look up in the index are **Darwin**, **natural selection**, **evolution**.

3

Solutions

A   Dry up

COPY

Water has different forms: **frozen** water, **liquid** water and water **vapour**.

Liquid water changes into water vapour when it is heated. A change like this is called **evaporation**.

Water vapour changes back into liquid water when it is cooled. This kind of change is called **condensation**.

Problem-solving competition

There's always a key to unlock any problem.

A puddle on the road disappears because the water evaporates. The water will evaporate more quickly on a hot or a windy day and when the water is spread out. Use these key ideas to solve the following problem as quickly as you can.

Problem

The last paper towel in the universe has fallen in a puddle. You have to dry the towel out as quickly as possible. You also have to complete a report sheet saying how you did this.

Your teacher will write down the time when you collect the wet paper towel. Timing will stop when you hand in the dry towel **and** a complete report.

Hints
- Talk about the problem with your partner.
- Plan your work before you collect the wet towel. Remember that timing starts when you collect it.
- Fill in as much of the report as you can before you start. This will save time.
- **Collect** any equipment you need **before** you collect the wet towel.
- Don't copy other people's ideas. They are probably not as good as your own.

Now solve the problem.

CHECKPOINT

B Rain down

It rains somewhere in Britain almost every day. It rains because water evaporates, rises into the air and then condenses.

Look at the picture below.

1 The picture shows the water cycle.
   a Describe what is happening.
   b Why do you think it is called a **cycle**?
2 Water also **freezes** and **melts**.
   Collect a copy of the diagram below. Fill in the missing words and stick the diagram into your book.

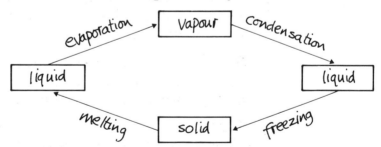

3 **Collect** a copy of the picture below. Stick it into your book. Write the word which describes what is happening to the water in each picture.

a

b

c

d

e

A Dissolving

Water is wonderful stuff. It can make things seem to disappear. Salt will disappear into water. So will sugar. This disappearing act is known as **dissolving**.

A substance that dissolves is **soluble**.

The substance that does the dissolving is a **solvent**.

Together, the solvent and the soluble substance make a **solution**.

Copy

> Sugar is **soluble** in the **solvent** hot water. It **dissolves** to give a sweet **solution**.

This diagram shows how to help sugar dissolve.

Another problem-solving competition

Use these ideas to solve the following problem as quickly as you can. Work with a partner.

You have to dissolve a blue crystal in two tablespoonsful of water as quickly as you can. You also have to complete a report sheet.

Don't dive in. Discuss the key to the problem with your partner first.

Your teacher will write down the time when you collect the crystal. Timing will stop when you hand in the solution and a complete report.
Read the hints for the problem on page 40.
Talk about the problem with your partner.
Now solve the problem.

B Testing solubility

Collect

Set of chemicals
Test-tube rack
Test tube
Wooden splint

1 Use one chemical at a time.
2 Add a small amount of the chemical to a test tube
   half full of water.
   Use just enough to cover the end of the wooden splint.

3 Shake the tube gently from side to side.
4 Decide if the chemical is soluble or insoluble. Put the
   result in a table like the one below.

chemical	Soluble or insoluble
Iron oxide	insoluble

Your teacher may show you the following experiment.

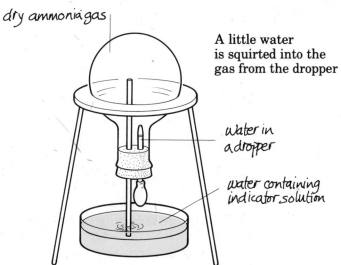

1 Describe what happened.
2 Is ammonia soluble or insoluble in water?

A Crystal clear

A solvent can get filled up with dissolved substance. The solution is **saturated** when no more of the substance can dissolve in it.

A saturated solution can be used to grow crystals. Remove some water (or cool the solution) and some of the dissolved substance has nowhere to go. It reappears as a solid.

Collect

Microscope
Slide
Cover slip
Dropper

1 Your teacher will show you how to set up the microscope.
Focus it carefully.

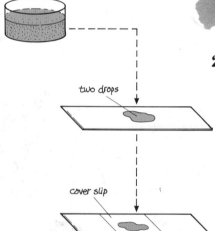

two drops

2 Take your slide and dropper to the hot saturated solution. Put two drops of the solution on the slide. Leave it on your bench for one minute.

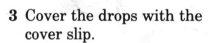

cover slip

3 Cover the drops with the cover slip.

4 Look at the slide under low-power magnification. Be patient. Wait for several minutes.

1 Describe what you did.
2 Make a large drawing of what you saw. (Draw the correct shape)
3 Use the pictures below to explain what you saw.

a lot of water holds a lot . . .

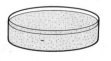

a little water holds a little . . .

CHECKPOINT

B   Grow slow

Crystals which grow slowly are usually bigger than crystals which grow quickly. Crystals will grow slowly from a cold saturated solution. They will grow quickly from a hot saturated solution as it cools.

small crystals

quick ►

◄ slow

large crystals

Collect

Bottle of alum
Test tube
Test tube rack
Wooden splint

You have to grow a huge crystal of alum using only half a test tube of water. The size of your crystal will be compared with the others in your class.

Think about
- the sentences at the top of this page
- the temperature of the water
- what to do with the solution to form crystals.

Discuss your ideas with your teacher, then start growing!

1 Describe what you did to grow the crystal.
2 Draw a diagram to show what you did. Label the diagram.
3 When the crystal is finished make a drawing of it in your book.
4 Who grew the biggest crystal in the class?
   How did you decide this crystal was the biggest?

CHECKPOINT

A The great ink stink

Chromatography is a way of separating some mixtures like inks or dyes.

One method is shown below.

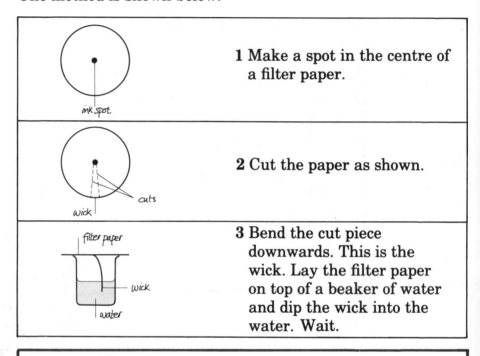

1 Make a spot in the centre of a filter paper.

ink spot

2 Cut the paper as shown.

wick   cuts

3 Bend the cut piece downwards. This is the wick. Lay the filter paper on top of a beaker of water and dip the wick into the water. Wait.

filter paper   wick   water

Collect

Card with message
Any equipment you need

Your problem is to discover who sent you a cheeky birthday card. Here are the suspects.

You have a pen from each suspect and some ink from the card. Use chromatography to discover the culprit.

Discuss • how to remove a sample of ink from the card
• how to compare this ink with suspects' pens.

Now solve the problem.

Write a report about your experiment. Your earlier problem report sheets will show you what to include. Stick the filter papers with your results into your book.

B Be a smartie

There are other ways of doing chromatography.

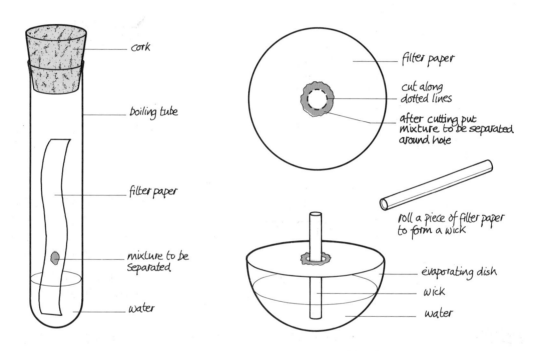

cork

boiling tube

filter paper

mixture to be separated

water

filter paper

cut along dotted lines

after cutting put mixture to be separated around hole

roll a piece of filter paper to form a wick

evaporating dish

wick

water

Collect

Spotting tile
Filter paper
Smartie (dark colour)
Small paint brush
Evaporating dish
or boiling tube,
rack and cork.

1 Put the Smartie on the tile and add **three** drops of water.

2 Brush the Smartie until the dye has dissolved in the water.

3 Use **one** of the methods above to find out if the dye is a single colour or a mixture of colours.

Write a report about the experiment. Your earlier problem report sheets will show you what to include.

Stick your filter paper into your book.

A Salt from rock

There are several methods of separating mixtures.

● **Filtering**—e.g. separating **sand** and **water**.

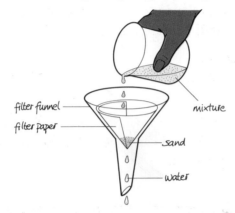

Sand is insoluble in water. It is caught by the filter paper. The water goes straight through.

filter funnel

filter paper

mixture

sand

water

● **Making crystals**—e.g. separating **salt** from **salty water**. Salt is soluble in water. As the water evaporates, the salt is left behind in the form of crystals.

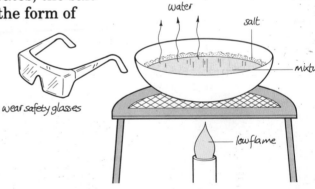

water

salt

mixture

wear safety glasses

low flame

● **Distillation**—e.g. separating **water** from **salty water**.

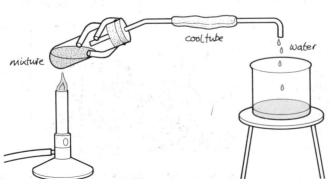

Salt is soluble in water. The water evaporates and goes through the tube. It is cooled in the tube and condenses back into water.

mixture

cool tube

water

Rock salt is salt from the ground. The salt is mixed with dirt and bits of rock. Your problem is to clean up the salt so that it is good enough to eat.

You will be given about 5 g of rock salt.
You have to produce as much clean dry salt from it as you can. You will be judged on

- time taken
- weight of salt
- whiteness of salt.

You can use any method or methods to separate the salt from the rock and dirt. You should only need basic laboratory equipment.

 Write a full report about your experiment.

B Separating quiz

Collect a copy of the pictures below. Name the method of separating mixtures which you would use to solve each of the problems.

1 Waiter, there's glass in my soup.

2 Waiter, water everywhere and not a drop to drink.

3 Waiter, all the sugar's dissolved in the wet bowl.

4 There's mud in the drinking water.

5 Which blue car has bumped into mine?

Filter builder

Your problem is to design and build a filter bed which will clean a sample of dirty water.

A filter bed is part of a water treatment plant. This is a diagram of a water treatment plant.

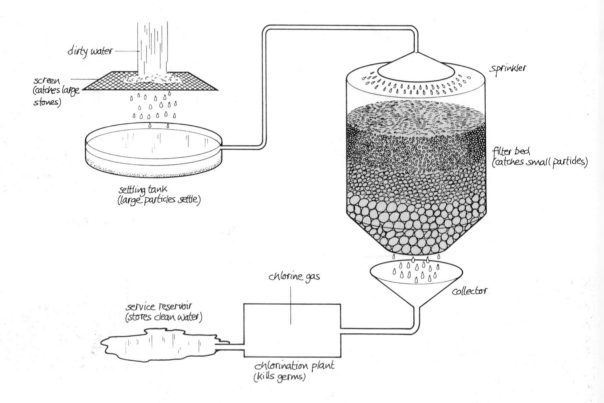

dirty water

screen
(catches large
stones)

settling tank
(large particles settle)

sprinkler

filter bed
(catches small particles)

collector

chlorine gas

service reservoir
(stores clean water)

chlorination plant
(kills germs)

Collect

Sample of dirty water
Plastic container
Collecting beaker
Gravel
Large pebbles
Sand
Small pebbles

Hints
• Look **carefully** at the diagram above.
• You are not allowed to use filter paper.
• You might have to try out several different designs before you find one that works well.

Now solve the problem.

Draw a labelled plan (or plans) of your design. You should also explain on the plan how your filter bed works.

Talkabout

Life in difficult places

What are the problems for living things in these places? How would you survive in them? What would you need?

Desert

Hot springs

Deep sea

Antarctic ice

Marie Curie

Marie Sklodowska was born in 1867 in Poland. Although she came from a poor family, she went to Paris to study science at the University. She was often hungry and cold, but she still managed to become the best student in her class.

She married a French physicist called Pierre Curie when she was 28. Together they worked with a rock called pitchblende. It was interesting because it gave out rays that could go through solid objects. They called these rays **radioactivity**. Marie Curie wanted to find out what was causing this radioactivity.

The Curies' laboratory was just a horrible damp shed. Nevertheless, after eight years, the two scientists managed to separate two new radioactive elements from the pitchblende. They called the two elements polonium (after Poland) and radium.

In 1906 Pierre Curie was knocked down in the road by a horse-drawn carriage and killed. Marie Curie went on to become a professor at the Sorbonne (a university in Paris). She won two Nobel prizes for science and her work became famous throughout the world.

One of the two elements that she discovered, radium, is now used to save many cancer patients. The radiation from radium kills the cancer cells.

 1 Copy and complete the personal history file about Marie Curie.

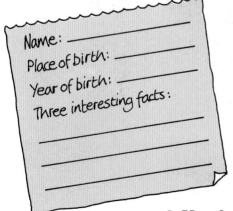

Name: _____

Place of birth: _____

Year of birth: _____

Three interesting facts:

_____

_____

_____

2 Use the books in the classroom or books from a library to find out more about Marie Curie and her work. Write a paragraph about what you find out. The key words to look up in the index are **Curie**, **radium**, **radiation**.

4

Science in action

A Energy in action

You need energy to make things happen. The cartoons below show six forms of energy in action.

a Heat energy

b Light energy

c Sound energy

d Electrical energy

e Stored energy

f Movement energy

The following two experiments show all the forms of energy in action.

1 Rub your finger very quickly along the table about 50 times.

2 Collect a battery, a bulb and two wires. Make the bulb light.

---

1 Describe what you did and what happened in each experiment.

2 What three forms of energy were involved in
- experiment 1
- experiment 2?

3 Copy this table. Use cartoons **a–f** to help you to complete it.

Name of the form of Energy		What it can do
a	Heat energy	Keep me warm
b		
c		
d		
e		
f		

CHECKPOINT

B Energy in hiding

1 Write down the title of each of the pictures below and the main form of energy that the picture shows.

a Windmill turning

b Breaking cup

c Electric bulb

d Loudspeaker

e Object up high

f Mains socket

g Fire

h Food

i Ice skater

j Sun

2 Write down the main form of energy that is hidden in each lettered line of the story.

The Visitor

a The winter sky was dark, clear and windless. The full moon cast an eery pale glow upon
b the shiny wet slates of the cottage roofs. An owl hooted and some unknown animal coughed in the shadows. There was nobody about, except Wally. Wally was the village baker.
c He baked all the local bread in a large ancient oven and he started work at 5 a.m. Wally was
d trudging slowly through the slush in the village square because he was carrying a sack of
e coal to work.
He was singing softly to himself . . . "Happy Christmas to me, Happy Christmas to me, Happy Christmas dear Wally . . ."
Suddenly there was a screech of brakes and a very large vehicle slid to a halt in front of him.
f Its headlamps were full on his face. Wally couldn't see a thing.

A gruff voice shouted out . . .
"Hey. Is this the village of 'Beef-on-Rye?' "
"Yes."
". . . and are you Wally Daker, the baker?"
"Yes."
"Well, Happy Christmas then."

The person in the vehicle threw down a heavy sack. It hit the ground with a thud just as
g the vehicle zoomed off over Wally's head. Wally opened the sack. Inside was a little yellow
h radio with new batteries, several kilograms of healthy food snacks and a large mail-order catalogue from Greenland. Wally switched the radio on, but not before he heard some jingle
i bells disappearing into the distance.

---

3 Complete the story with one sentence in which **sound** energy is hidden.

Changing the form

A Energy for a change

Energy can make things happen. Something only happens when energy changes from one form into another form.

A bunsen burner uses gas.
The gas has **stored energy**.

The burning gas makes heat.
The stored energy of the gas
has changed into **heat
energy**.

Some stored energy also
changes into **light energy**.

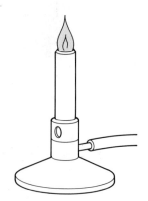

We can write this as an energy change.

Starting energy   *Finishing energy*
Stored   ⟶   Heat and light.

Collect a report sheet. Write the energy change for each experiment that you finish.

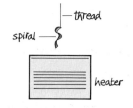

1 Hold the spiral
above the heater
with the thread.

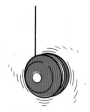

2 Make the yo-yo go.

3 Press the switch.

4 Wind up the toy and
let it go.

5 Pluck the strings.

6 Switch on the disco
strobe.

CHECKPOINT

B More energy changes

Copy and complete the table.

Picture	What is happening	Starting energy	Finishing energy
a			
b			
c			

Energy dominoes

Play dominoes in the usual way but match the picture with the written energy change.

Copy and complete the sketch of the domino game below. Make up your **own** linking domino.

stored to heat		? What energy change has happened?	? Draw a suitable diagram	stored to heat	

57

4.3 *The machine scene*

A The reel wheel

A machine is an energy changer. A machine changes one form of energy into another more useful form.

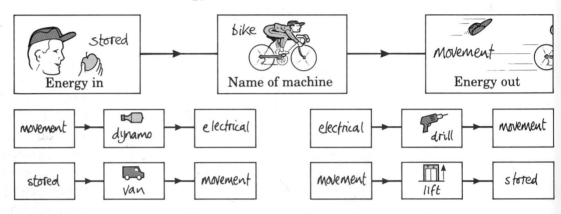

Collect

Reel wheel kit

The picture below shows a machine called a **reel wheel**. It changes the stored energy in an elastic band into movement energy.

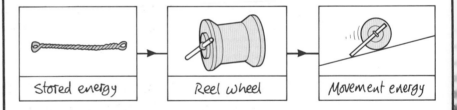

Make a reel wheel. Use the picture above as a guide. Race your reel wheel against a few others in the class.

1 What is a machine? Give two examples from this page. Write down the energy change for each example.
2 Write a full report about making the reel wheel. Include the following:

> Name of machine
>
> How the machine works
>
> The main energy change in the machine

B Big machines

Your teacher will show you a big machine; perhaps a steam engine like this.

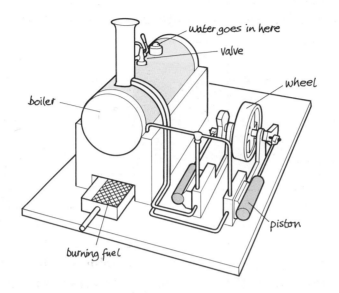

Discuss
How does the machine work? What are the important energy changes when the machine is working? (There are at least three energy changes.)

---

1 Go to one of the machines set up in the room.
2 Read the instruction card carefully.
3 Make the machine work and study it.

---

1 Write a report about each of the machines that you study. You should include sentences about
  • how the machine works
  • the important energy changes when it is working.
2 Copy and complete the table for the machines **a–d**.

Picture	Name of machine	Important energy changes
a		

a

b

c

d

CHECKPOINT

A The body machine

You know that • there are different forms of energy
 • a machine changes one form of energy into a more useful form.
Your body is a kind of machine.

Energy in		Energy out
?	→	?

Do this experiment.

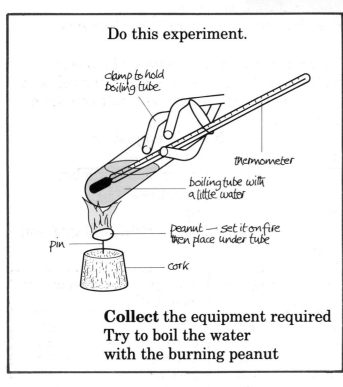

clamp to hold boiling tube

thermometer

boiling tube with a little water

Peanut — set it on fire then place under tube

pin

cork

Collect the equipment required
Try to boil the water
with the burning peanut

CAN I SWIM? c

LOOK OUT!! a

d

a Noisy throat. S____energy

b Powerful muscle. M____energy

c Thoughtful energy. E____energy

d Tubby tummy. S____energy

e Sweaty body. H____energy

1 Draw a diagram of the experiment.
2 Describe what happened in the experiment.
3 Name the form of energy that goes into your body if you eat a peanut.
4 Make a table with two columns. Label the first column 'Part of body' and the second column 'Form of energy out'.
By looking at the cartoon above complete the table.

CHECKPOINT

B Energy from food

Watch the demonstration experiment.

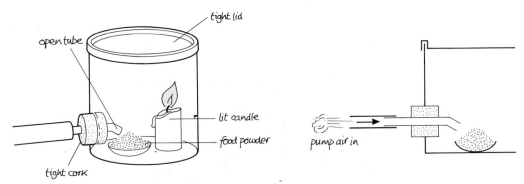

1 Draw a labelled diagram to show what happens next.
2 What form of energy does food contain?
3 How do you know from this experiment that food has energy?
4 The amount of energy in food varies. Energy in food is measured in kilojoules or in calories. Use the table below to work out how much energy you would take in if you ate a meal of average helpings of

a cream soup
   2 sausage rolls
   baked beans
   chips
   ice cream and jelly

b whole grapefruit
   cottage cheese
   lettuce and cucumber
   2 tomatoes
   apple

5 Use the table below to work out a meal which will give you about 3500 kilojoules.

Average helping of	kilojoules	Average helping of	kilojoules	Average helping of	kilojoules
sausage roll	1680	cheddar cheese	920	jelly	300
pizza	1260	cottage cheese	120	brussel sprouts	80
beef curry	1260	lemonade	760	cucumber	20
chicken	840	tea, milk, sugar	210	potatoes	380
fish finger	210	cornflakes	420	crisps	530
scrambled egg	500	porridge	630	peas	80
haddock	500	rice	500	thick veg soup	630
apple	210	spaghetti	420	baked beans	1470
banana	300	milk	630	carrots	80
grapefruit	120	yoghurt	590	lettuce	20
apple pie	840	jam/marmalade	380	chips	1130
custard	630	slice of bread	420	tomato	40
ice cream	500	pat of butter	210		
rice pudding	720	cream soup	840		

CHECKPOINT

Writeabout electricity

Electricity matters

How was electricity discovered, how is it made, how is it put to work and how is it used sensibly?

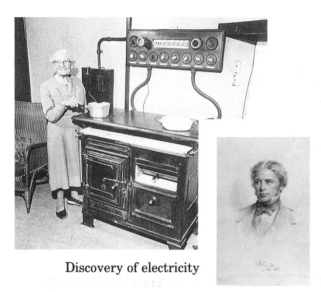

Discovery of electricity

Making electricity

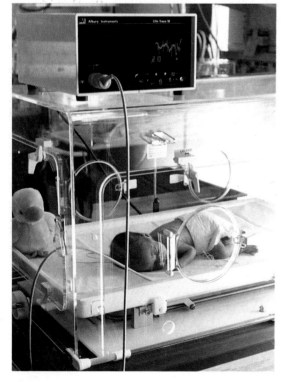

Working with electricity

Using electricity sensibly

Project outline
Your writing projects should always be
- in your own words
- about things that are interesting
- neat
- in complete sentences

You can include
- coloured diagrams
- cut-out pictures
- graphs and bar charts
- newspaper clippings

You can find information in
- newspapers
- library books
- science books
- electricity-board leaflets

Pick **at least two** of the following topics. Your teacher will tell you how much time you have. Write as much as you can about your topics in this time.

Topic	Think about including
1 Discovery of electricity	Important events Important people Important dates
2 Making electricity	Coal, oil and nuclear Hydroelectric Wind and wave Solar and geothermal
3 Working with electricity	In the home In the school In the factory and office
4 Using electricity sensibly	Safety Wasting electricity Saving electricity Future uses

Albert Einstein

Albert Einstein was born in Germany in 1879. He did not enjoy school very much. After going to Zurich Polytechnic, he went to work for the Swiss Patent Office (a patent is a description of a new invention).

While he was there, he did a lot of thinking about the way things move. At the age of 26 he wrote about his thinking. His work was a great success and it was talked about all over the world.

Albert Einstein described the movement of objects as being relative and so his theory was called the theory of relativity. He worked out that the speed of light was the fastest possible speed in the universe. Light travels about 300 000 kilometres every second. Light can therefore travel from London to Edinburgh and back 250 times in one second.

He also worked out that there was a connection between mass and energy. The equation $E=mc^2$ describes this. This discovery led to the development of the atomic bomb and nuclear reactors.

Albert Einstein's work has also been important in modern mathematics and astronomy. His ideas predicted some amazing results. For example, did you know that you increase in mass as you move faster? So when you run for the bus you get heavier! Did you know that time goes faster when you stand still? So if you are on a ride at the fair then you are getting older more slowly than the friend who is watching you! However, on earth, these changes in mass and time are very tiny. You will never notice them.

Name: _____
Place of birth: _____
Year of birth: _____
Three interesting facts:
_____
_____
_____

1 Copy and complete the personal history file about Albert Einstein.

2 Use the books in the classroom or books from a library to find out more about Albert Einstein and his work. Write a paragraph about what you find out. The key words to look up in the index are **Einstein**, **relativity**, **speed of light**.

5

Scale skills

A   Measurement scales

People have always needed to measure quantities like mass, length, time, volume and temperature.

Balance

Body

Hourglass

Bushel

Elbow

These methods of measurement were not very exact. Today we use more accurate instruments.

Balance	Metre rule	Clock	Measuring cylinder	Thermometer

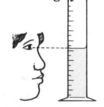

Mass (weight) in grams (g) — Length in centimetres (cm) — Time in seconds (s) — Volume in cubic centimetres (cm^3) — Temperature in degrees Celsius (°C)

You can compare modern and historical measurements of length.

Measure the length of the bench
  a   in centimetres (with a metre rule)
  b   in hands (with your hand)
  c   in hands (with your partner's hand).

Record your results in a table.

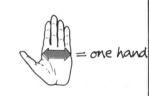
= one hand

---

1 Collect and complete a copy of the modern scales diagram.

2 Why is it better to measure with a metre rule rather than a hand?

Make and record the following measurements using the correct modern instruments.

Check your answers with your teacher's checklist.

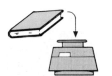  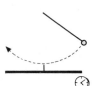

a Mass of a book   **b** Width of a milk bottle   **c** Time of a swing   **d** How much a bottle holds   **e** Temperature of ice

B Measurement puzzles

1 What is the reading at each arrow?

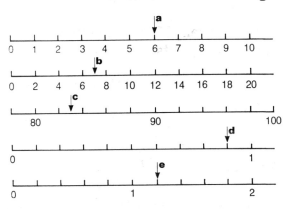 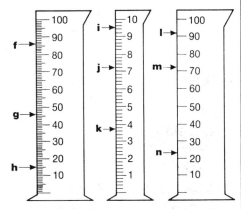

2 Make and record the following measurements using the correct modern instruments.

a Mass of a milk bottle   **b** Height of your seat   **c** Time to write your name five times

d Volume of a carton   **e** Temperature of tap water

A Body measurements

Everyone's body is different. This means that your body has a special **body plan**. It has its own measurements.

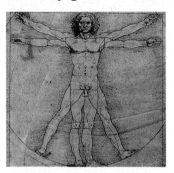

16th century body plan

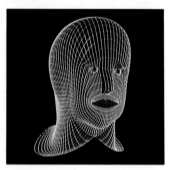

20th century body plan

1 **Collect** a body plan.
2 Make all the measurements below on your own body. Record each measurement on your body plan.

a Height (cm)
b Waist (cm)
c Mass (kg)
d Temperature (°C)

e Holding breath (s)

f Pulse rate (beats every minute)

g Reaction time (s)

h Volume of air breathed out in a **normal** breath (L)

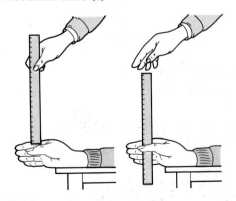

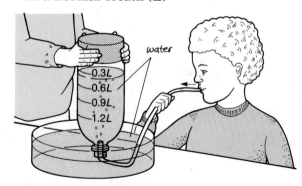

water

1 Hold your hand out straight.
2 Your partner will hold a ruler at the top of your open hand and then drop it.
3 You must catch the ruler as quickly as possible.
4 Find your reaction time from the chart.

1 Breath out into the jar.
2 Read the scale on the jar to find out the volume of air that you have breathed out.

CHECKPOINT

B Body building

Hamish was famished. He had been trapped on an island for ages. All he could catch was a small and unusual animal. Luckily Hamish was a good scientist. Before he ate this rare animal, he recorded some of its measurements. Here they are.

Part of animal	Measurement
body	mass 20g
2 front legs	length 6cm
1 back leg	length 5cm
head	volume 10cm³
tail	length 8cm
nose	mass 2g

Make an accurate model of the animal. Your measurements should be the same as those in the table.

Use plasticine for the body, the head and the nose. Use straws for the legs. Use string for the tail. Put a smile on the face of the animal.

1 Draw an accurate picture of your animal.
2 Measure and record on your drawing
   a the length of the body
   b the height from the ground to the top of its head
   c the total mass of the animal.

A Making bar graphs

Scientists make different kinds of measurements.

Height

Single measurement

Height varies in a group

Group measurement

Height changes with age

Changing measurement

Height is affected by a number of things

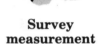

Survey measurement

You have been practising making **single measurements**. You will now make **group measurements**.

Hair colour and hand use are two examples of group measurements that you can make in your class.

1 a There are three hair colour groups: **light**, **dark** and **red**. Count the number of people in each group.

b Collect a sheet of graph paper. Draw a bar graph of your results. Use the hints below to help you.

Make the graph as big as possible. Put the numbers in, evenly spaced.

Give each group the same space on the bottom line.

Draw a bar for each group up to the number of people in the group; e.g. 5 people have light hair.

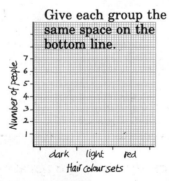
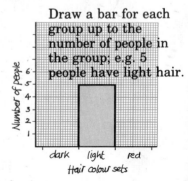

2 Collect another sheet of graph paper. Draw a bar graph to show whether people in your class can write with their left hand, their right hand or both.

CHECKPO

B Reading graphs

1 Look at the **bar graph** below.

Bar graph showing the variation in **shoe size** in a group of people

    a What is the most common shoe size?
    b What is the least common shoe size?
    c How many people have size 6 shoes?
    d What is the biggest shoe size in this group?
    e How many people had their shoe size measured?

2 A **pie chart** is another way of showing group measurement. Look at the pie chart below.

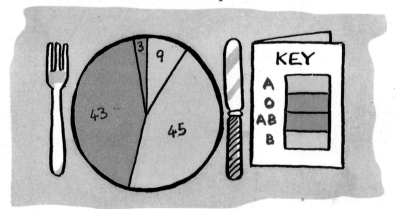

Pie chart showing the number of people of each **blood group** in an office.

    a How many blood groups are there?
    b What is the most common blood group?
    c What is the least common blood group?
    d How many people have blood group A?
    e How many people had their blood group tested?

Problem

Conduct a survey

Your problem is to find out what the people in your school think about **one** of these topics:

Favourite foods

TV programmes

Exercise

You have to design and use a survey. Your survey form should be like this one.

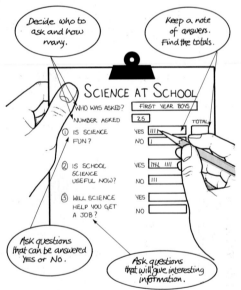

1 Write five questions for your survey.
2 Ask at least 20 people to answer each of the questions.
3 Count the **yes** and **no** answers for each question.
4 Present the results as five bar graphs, one for each question.
5 Use colour to make your graphs attractive and easier to understand.

Graph stories

What story do you think these graphs tell us?

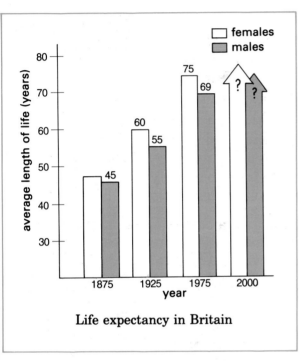

Life expectancy in Britain

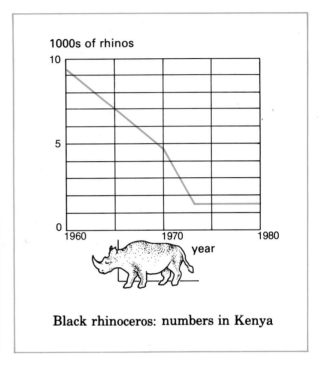

Black rhinoceros: numbers in Kenya

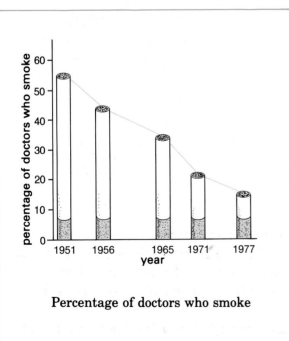

Percentage of doctors who smoke

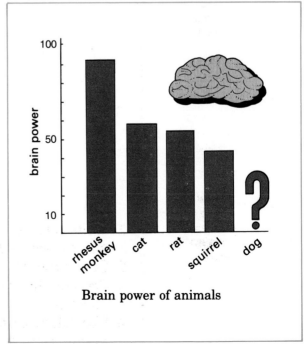

Brain power of animals

Aristotle

Aristotle was born in Greece in 384 BC. His parents died when he was young. He attended the famous academy in Athens to study and showed an interest in many different things. Aristotle was very observant. Like you, he tried to be exact in his descriptions of what he saw. Most important, when Aristotle saw something happen, he wanted to know the cause of it.

What ideas did this great man work out? He thought that the world was round. He also thought that the stars and planets moved around the earth and tried to explain this movement. Some of his best work was done in biology. He named over 500 different animals and tried to classify all living things into sets. He wrote the first full descriptions of lions and elephants.

Aristotle described many marine (sea) creatures. The mouth of a sea urchin is still known as Aristotle's purse. He also studied bees and knew how they behaved in a hive. Beekeepers expect to get stung from time to time. Perhaps this is how Aristotle found out how a bee sting works.

As well as being an astronomer and a zoologist, Aristotle was also interested in mathematics, botany and medicine. There was hardly a branch of science in which he didn't do important work. Many of his ideas were accepted for over 2000 years. What a brilliant man!

Name: _____
Place of birth: _____
Year of birth: _____
Three interesting facts:
_____
_____
_____

 1 Copy and complete the personal history file about Aristotle.

2 Use the books in the classroom or books from a library to find out more about Aristotle and his work. Write a paragraph about what you find out. The key words to look up in the index are **Aristotle, Greek science, astronomy, classification**.

6
Light thoughts

6.1 *Electric problems*

A A light difficulty

Copy

> Electricity is safe if you are careful. It is dangerous if you misuse it.
>
> **Always** • use a proper plug with mains sockets
> • use a power pack or a battery for circuit work.
>
> Electricity can move through wires and many other objects. We call the path it takes a **circuit**.

To make it easier to draw a picture of a circuit each part of the circuit is represented by a different symbol. For example:

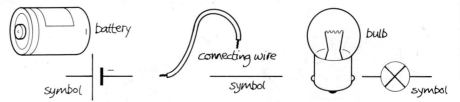

This unit is all about problem solving. We will look at
• **repair** problems
• **design** problems.

If your radio stops working then you have a repair problem to solve. You have to mend the radio.

If you want to protect your house from burglars then you have a design problem to solve. You have to make an alarm.

Both types of problems should be solved in a sensible way, in steps.

For example, Disco Denver needs to mend his broken disco lights. He solves this repair problem in a sensible way.

1 What type of problem is it? 2 Any ideas on what to do? 3 What's the best idea? 4 How do you try it out? 5 Did it work?

Solve the following design problem by using the same problem-solving steps as Disco Denver.

Problem: to make two bulbs shine as brightly as possible.

Complete each stage of the problem planner. Stick it into your book.

B Sort the problems

There are **repair** and **design** problems. In each example below write down what the problem is **and** what type of problem it is. You will have to build circuits 7 and 8.

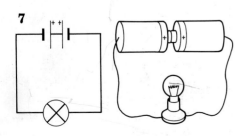

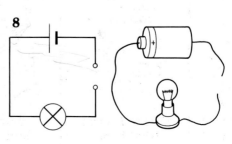

A Flexitime

Copy

> Some materials let electricity go through them. They are called **conductors**. Some don't. They are called **insulators**.

Electricity can be dangerous and yet we use it at home. The electricity is **conducted** by wire. How can we use wire in our homes safely? This design problem has been solved in a simple way.

Collect and examine a piece of wire.

Copy the following diagram. What is the design problem that has to be solved before this wire can be used in the house?

Collect

Parts needed to build circuit
Bag of materials

1 Look at the circuit diagram.

2 Use the circuit to find out which materials are conductors and which materials are insulators. The material should fill the gap in the circuit.

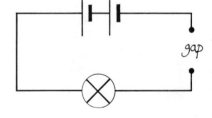

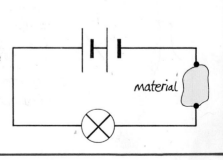

1 Draw a diagram of the circuit you built.
   Explain how this circuit was used to sort out conductors from insulators.
2 Make a table of your results. Your table should have two columns.
3 What kind of substances are conductors?
4 **Collect** and examine a piece of flex. Flex like this is used to wire a house safely.
   Copy the following diagram. How is the flex designed to be safe?

B Faulty circuit

To solve a problem you first decide what type of problem it is. You then come up with ideas on what to do. At this stage it is important to think of **lots** of ideas.

There is no electricity going round this circuit.
The repair problem is caused by a faulty bulb.

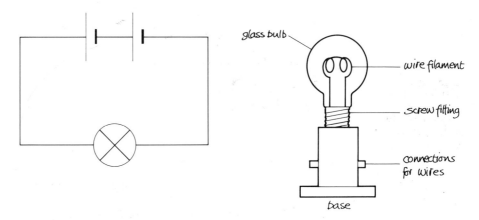

1 Look at the drawing of the bulb. Write a list of all the possible faults in your book.
2 Write down some ideas on what to do to solve the problem. (Go through your list of faults as you answer this question.)
3 Collect the circuit with the faulty bulb. Try out your ideas. What fault was causing the problem?

A   A switch in time

Copy

> Electricity flows around a circuit. This flow is called a **current**. The current goes through some materials (such as copper) more easily than others (such as water). Water has a higher **resistance** than copper. When resistance is high, the current is low.

The idea of resistance helps us to solve some circuit design problems. For example,
- to make a switch to turn the current on and off (simple switch)
- to make a switch to raise and lower the current (dimmer switch).

Collect

Switches
Metal foil
or ring pull tops
Bulb
Battery
4 connecting wires
2 crocodile clips

Collect

Parts needed to build the dimmer switch
Copper wire
Nichrome wire

1 Look at the switch. Find out what happens inside the switch when it operates.

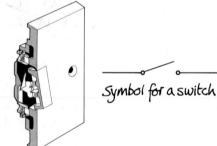

Symbol for a switch

2 Design and build a circuit with a simple switch in it.

3 A dimmer switch makes a bulb dimmer by increasing the resistance to the current. Build the circuit below.

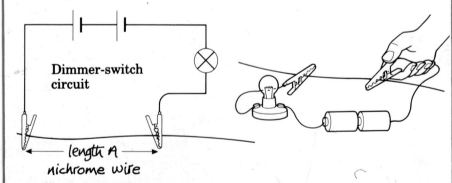

Dimmer-switch circuit

length A
nichrome wire

a Find out what happens when you change the length of the wire (length A).
b Find out what happens when you replace the nichrome wire with copper wire. Keep length A the same each time.

Write a report about your investigation of the dimmer-switch circuit. Include

- **Title**
  What were you investigating?
- **Method**
  What did you do?
- **Results**
  What happened to the brightness of the bulb when you changed
    (i) the length of wire?
    (ii) the type of wire?
- **Conclusion**
  When is resistance to current high?

B TV repair

When you know the type of problem and you have some ideas for solving it, then you have to pick the best idea to try out first.

Imagine that you have the following repair problem. Your TV picture suddenly disappears while you are watching. The table shows three things that might need repairing and some ideas for fixing each one.

Pick the best idea to try out **first** for each repair. Write the idea down and a reason for your choice.

Might need repair	Ideas to try out
1 Plug 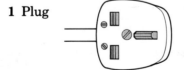	**a** Replace the fuse. **b** Change the flex. **c** Rewire the house. **d** Check the plug is in the socket. **e** Check the socket is on.
2 Aerial 	**a** Climb onto the roof to check it. **b** Check that the aerial lead is plugged into the TV. **c** Check for a broken aerial lead. **d** Replace the aerial. **e** Move the TV to a different room.
3 TV 	**a** Buy a new TV. **b** Adjust the volume control. **c** Shake the TV. **d** Adjust the controls at the back of the TV. **e** Change the channel selector.

A House lighting

Copy

There are two important ways of connecting bulbs in a circuit:

●in **series**

The bulbs are all in a single row

●in **parallel**

The bulbs are in branches

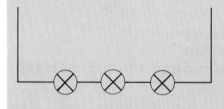 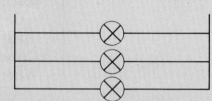

One of these ways of connecting bulbs is used to solve important design problems in your home.

In your home you want
- **bright** lights
- lights that **stay on** even when one bulb breaks or is removed.

Collect

Parts needed to build circuit

1 Build a series circuit and a parallel circuit, using two batteries in each.
2 Find out which circuit would be better for house lights.

Write about your experiment(s). Include

- **Title**
- **Method**
  Details of what you did
- **Results**
  Details of what you found out
- **Conclusion**
  Explain which circuit is better for house lighting

CHECKPOINT

B Trying solutions

You know what type of problem it is and you've chosen what you hope is the best idea for solving it. Now you need to try out that idea.

Here is a sensible way to try out an idea:
- decide **how** to try it out (method)
- decide **what** you need to collect (equipment)
- **try out** your idea.

1 What is a sensible way of trying out a problem-solving idea?

2 Nick has a repair problem. His radio-cassette player isn't recording properly. He has several ideas about how to fix it. For each idea, put the pictures in the order which shows the best way of trying the idea out.

a Fit new batteries

b Ask his friend to fix it.

A Wire a plug

Copy

The electricity supply from an electrical socket can be dangerous. **Do not put a test plug into a socket.**

Collect

Test plug
Screwdriver
Three-core flex
Wire strippers (your teacher will show you how to use these)

1 Examine the test plug and the flex. Find the important parts.

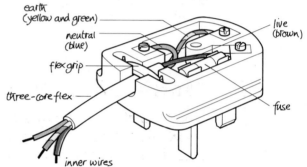

earth (yellow and green)
neutral (blue)
flex grip
three-core flex
inner wires
live (brown)
fuse

2 Strip about 5 cm of the outer cover of the flex.
    Do not cut through the cover of the inner wires.
3 Put the flex under the cord grip.
    Tighten the screws of the cord grip.
4 Cut about 2 cm off the brown covered and the blue covered wires.
5 Strip about 0.5 cm of the plastic cover from the three wires.
6 Put the bare wires into the correct terminals like those in the picture.
    Remember: BRown goes to Bottom Right
    BLue goes to Bottom Left
    Third green/yellow wire goes to Top.
7 Tighten the terminal screws.
8 Check your wiring with your teacher.

1 Copy and complete the table.

	Name of terminal		
	Neutral	Live	Earth
Where it is			
Colour of wire			

2 What is the cord grip for?
3 Why is the main part of the plug made of plastic?
4 What should be done to correct each of the these faulty
situations?

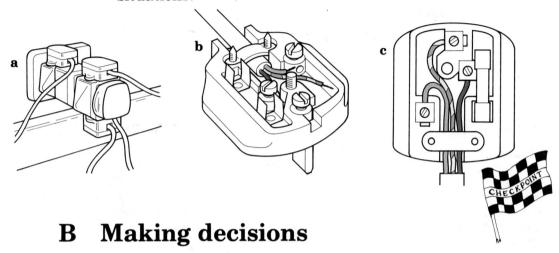

B Making decisions

The final stage in solving a problem is to decide when to stop
trying out ideas. You stop when your idea works well. The
idea does not have to be perfect but you must be satisfied that
the problem is under control.

Decide whether you would be satisfied with these results.
Explain your answer.

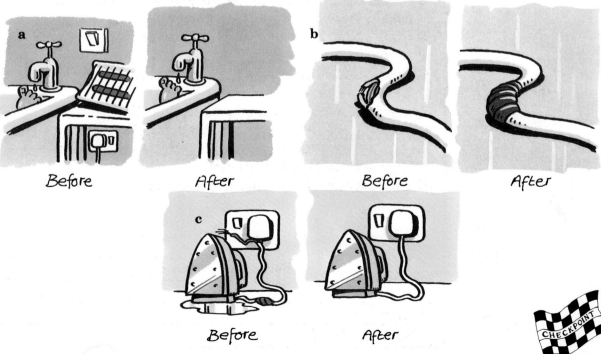

Before   After   Before   After

Before   After

Static electricity

A Static problems

The word **static** is often used in connection with electricity. Here are some examples of static electricity.

You know that static electricity is there because it can

- •make things move
- •move itself.

Do each of these six experiments.

a Paper and comb

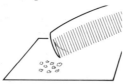

Rub the comb on wool. Bring it close to small bits of paper.

b Rod and water

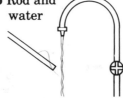

Use a trickle of water. Rub the rod. Bring it close to the water.

c TV crackle

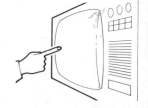

Turn the TV on. Bring your finger close to the screen.

d Sticky balloon

Rub the balloon on a jersey. Put it on the wall.

e Warm nylon

Put on a nylon shirt. Blow hot air over it with a hair dryer. Take the shirt off quickly.

f Van de Graaff machine

Your teacher will show you some experiments.

For each experiment
- write a title
- describe what you did
- explain how you know that static electricity was present.

B Static solutions

Static electricity sometimes causes design problems.

The pictures show some static-electricity problems and hint at how they are solved. For each example state the problem and describe the solution.

Problem   *Solution*

Static electicity in an operating theatre attracts dirt and bacteria.

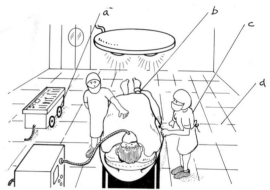

Lightning can cause fire in a building.

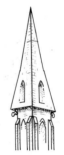

Static electricity at a petrol pump could set the petrol on fire.

A Beat the burglar

Many people worry about burglars. They ask 'What can we do to keep the burglars out of our home?' You are going to use scientific problem solving to help such people.

Discuss
- What type of problem do you have?
- Any ideas on what to do?
- What's the best idea?
- How do you try it out?

Stage 1
List all the possible ways that burglars can get into homes. These cause design problems.

Stage 2
Pick one of the design problems. Think up ideas for preventing the burglars getting in this way. Write down your ideas.

Stage 3
Choose the best idea. Give a reason for choosing this one.

Stage 4
Describe a way of trying out your idea. Include a drawing.

> Using your knowledge of electricity, design and build an alarm which turns on a warning light when a burglar opens a window. Ask your teacher for the equipment that you need.

How satisfied are you with your alarm?

A world without electricity

Imagine a world without electricity.
Take away the electricity from each picture below.
- What would the problems be?
- How would you solve them?

Electricity for heating

Electricity for lighting

Electricity for communication

Electricity for transport

Alessandro Volta

Alessandro Volta was an Italian. He was born in 1745. At this time, electricity was a mystery. Most people thought it was a form of magic and they gave themselves static shocks to cure illness. Alessandro Volta invented a machine which could give quite a big shock.

Alessandro Volta got a job as a university professor. He became interested in the discovery that two metals could make a dead frog's leg twitch. Another scientist called Galvani thought that this twitching was caused by electricity produced by the leg. Alessandro Volta disagreed. He used experiments to show that the twitching only occurred when the frog's leg was placed between the two metals, and the two metals were connected together.

In 1799 he built a big pile of copper and zinc discs which gave out electricity. This was the first chemical battery. Volta continued to improve his invention. He made batteries that gave out a high current. He made batteries that other scientists could learn from.

Napoleon was so impressed that he made Alessandro Volta a Count. Count Volta's name lives on in the electrical unit called the **volt**.

1 Copy and complete the personal history file about Alessandro Volta.

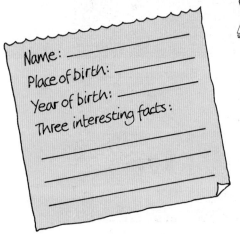

Name: _____
Place of birth: _____
Year of birth: _____
Three interesting facts:
_____
_____
_____
_____

2 Use the books in the classroom or books from a library to find out more about Volta and his work. Write a paragraph about what you find out. The key words to look up in the index are **Volta, battery, Galvani, volt**.

7

Small beginnings

A   Microscope parts

Your eyes need help to see very small things. A microscope magnifies small things, making them appear bigger. There are different kinds of microscopes.

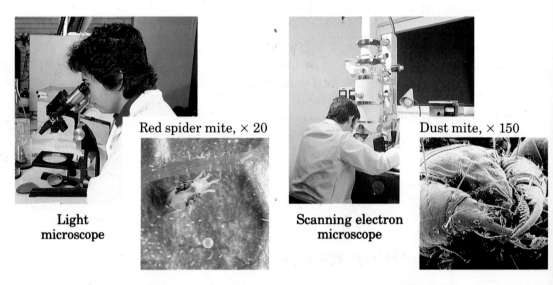

Red spider mite, × 20

Light microscope

Dust mite, × 150

Scanning electron microscope

You are going to use a light microscope like this.

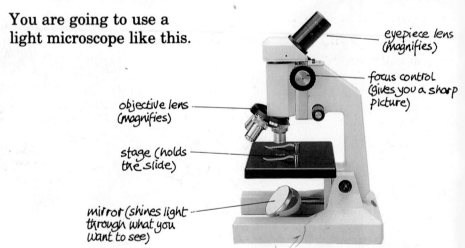

eyepiece lens (magnifies)

focus control (gives you a sharp picture)

objective lens (magnifies)

stage (holds the slide)

mirror (shines light through what you want to see)

A light microscope will magnify things. Light is shone through the object so that you can see it. The object must therefore be very thin.

1   **Collect** a diagram of the light microscope and stick it into your book. Complete the diagram by adding labels. Read and learn the rules on the diagram.
2   Make a table of two columns in your book to show the **parts** of the microscope and what each part **does**.

1 **Collect** slide A. Focus the microscope on the slide. Watch the letter when you move the slide up/down and left/right.

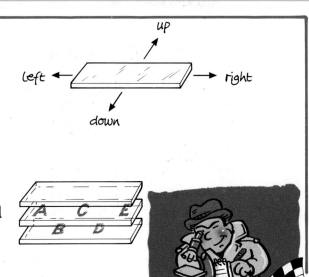

   a What is the letter on slide A?
   b Describe how the letter moves.

2 **Collect** slide B. There is a word on slide B. It has five letters. The first letter is on the second slide down, find this. The next letter is on the last slide, find this. Focus up, then down, then up again to read the next three letters.

What is the word on the slide?

B Using a microscope

1 **Collect** a fibre slide. Use the microscope and the drawings below to identify your fibre.

Draw your fibre. Name it.

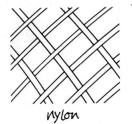
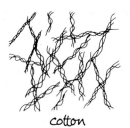
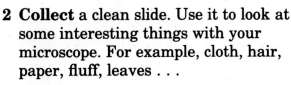

nylon   cotton

2 **Collect** a clean slide. Use it to look at some interesting things with your microscope. For example, cloth, hair, paper, fluff, leaves . . .

Make a large drawing of everything that you look at.

A Cells

About 300 years ago Robert Hooke made an important discovery using a miscroscope. You are going to see what he discovered. First you must know how to prepare a microscope slide. Your teacher will show you how.

Collect

Microscope
Slide and cover slip
Dropper bottle of iodine stain
Thin piece of onion skin

1 Make a slide of a thin piece of onion skin.

Describe how you prepared the slide.

place thin skin on a microscope slide

add a drop of water

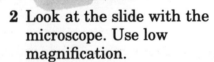

lower a cover slip onto the onion skin

it should look like this

2 Look at the slide with the microscope. Use low magnification.

Look for a pattern on the slide. What does the pattern look like?

3 Add one drop of iodine stain to the slide. Replace the cover slip. Look at the slide again. Use a higher magnification.

Iodine helps to show more clearly that plants are made of tiny units called **cells.** Draw two of the cells. Show as much detail as you can.

Copy

Some very small plants and animals have only one cell, but most plants and animals are made up of many cells. Cells are very small. In one cubic millimetre of human blood there are more than five million cells!

A living cell has different parts which do different jobs.

Most cells have

1 membrane which controls the movement of substances in and out of the cell

2 cytoplasm where chemical changes take place

3 nucleus which controls the cell

  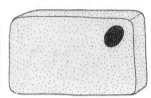

Most plant cells also have

4 cell wall which gives the cell shape and support

5 chloroplasts which make food using sunlight

6 vacuole which holds a watery solution

  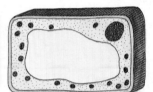

1 **Collect** a cells diagram and stick it into your book. Label all the important parts of the animal cell and the plant cell.
2 Copy and complete the table below.

Part of the cell	What the part does
1.	
2.	

B More cells

1 Make a slide of the green plant material.
2 Look at the slide using the microscope.

Draw two of the plant cells. Label six important parts of the cells in your drawing.

7.3 Special cells

A Cell types

Copy

Most living things contain different types of cells. Each type does a different job.

Collect

Microscope slide
Cover slip
Slice of plant stem
Bottle of stain

1 Make a slide of the plant stem. Add a drop of stain.
2 Look at the stem under the microscope using low magnification.
3 Find three different types of cell.

look here (cells for protection)

look here (cells for carrying water)

look here (cells for support)

How an expert cuts a slide from a plant stem

4 Draw the shape of each cell in your book. Write down the job that each cell does. Give your drawing a title.

Your body also has different types of cells. Some of these are shown below.

Sex cell
A sex cell carries information. A male makes sex cells called sperm. A female makes sex cells called eggs

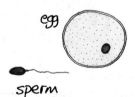
egg
sperm

Heart muscle cell
A heart muscle cell makes the heart beat.

Brain cell
A brain cell passes information on through its connections.

Motor nerve cell
A motor nerve cell controls movement. It passes a message from the brain to a muscle.

White blood cell
A white blood cell fights disease.

Skin cell
A skin cell forms part of a layer which protects the body.

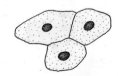

1 Name six different types of human body cell.
2 Choose two types of human body cell.
   Use the information available to
   find out about your chosen cells.
   a List three important facts about
   each of your chosen cells.
   b Draw the cells.

B Sex cells

Look at the photograph of human sex cells.

Human egg
with sperms
(× 400 approximately)

Only one egg is
usually released
at a time. Many millions
of sperm are released
at a time.

Copy and complete the following table.

	Human sperm	Human egg
Shape (draw)		
Size		
Number		

1 Your teacher will give you two slides to look at. One is
   of pollen (which contains the male sex cells of a plant).
   The other is of ovules (which contain the female sex
   cells of a plant).
2 Look at the pollen under the microscope. Draw and
   label what you see. Write down one word to describe
   • shape of pollen
   • size of pollen
   • how many pollen.
3 Repeat with the slide of the ovules. Draw and
   describe the ovules this time.

Making new life

A Animal reproduction

Every living thing must reproduce. In most animals sexual reproduction takes place. The diagram shows the important events in the reproduction of a stickleback. Vertebrates all have the same pattern of events. The details of what happens during each event may be different.

Important event	*What happens*
Maturity Female swollen with eggs Male with red breast	The animal makes sperm or eggs. The animal is only now able to reproduce. It is an adult.
Courtship and mating Female lays eggs in a nest Male follows the female and spreads sperm over the eggs	The male and the female meet. This is courtship. The male sperm is put near the female egg cell. This is mating.
Fertilisation magnified many times	The sperm enters the egg cell. This happens outside the female body in most fish and amphibians. It happens inside the body in reptiles, birds and mammals.
Embryo growth	The fertilised egg divides and grows to form an embryo. The embryo contains thousands of cells.
Birth	The baby animal is born. In many animals it hatches from an egg. In mammals it comes directly from the mother's body.
Growth	The baby animal gets bigger. It grows into a mature adult.

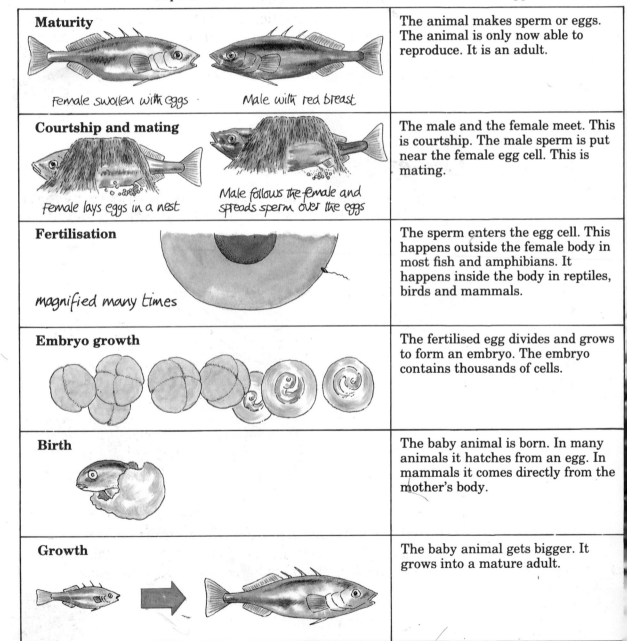

1 **Collect** a summary of this diagram and complete it. Stick it into your book.

2 Copy the following passage. Put the words on the left in the correct place in the passage.

egg sexual asexual

dogs frogs born

grows outside

inside reproduce

adult

There are two kinds of reproduction, sexual and _____ reproduction. Fertilisation occurs during _____ reproduction when the sperm meets the _____. In some animals such as humans and _____ fertilisation happens _____ the body of the female. In other animals such as _____ and fish, fertilisation happens _____ the body of the female. The fertilised egg _____ into a baby animal and is _____. The baby grows to maturity and becomes an _____. The animal is now ready to _____.

CHECKPOINT

B Life cycles

Look at the pictures below. They show some important events in the life cycle of a turtle, but the order of events is mixed up.

Write down the correct order of events

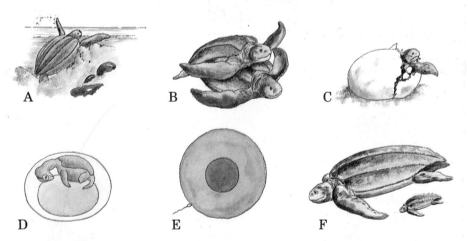

A

B

C

D

E

F

Collect

Die
Timer
Life Cycles
information sheet

Now play the game Life Cycles. This game involves sorting out the life cycles of a fish, a frog and a chicken. The information sheet explains how to play the game

CHECKPOINT

A Plant reproduction

The diagram shows some important events in the sexual life of a flowering plant. All these events are part of reproduction.

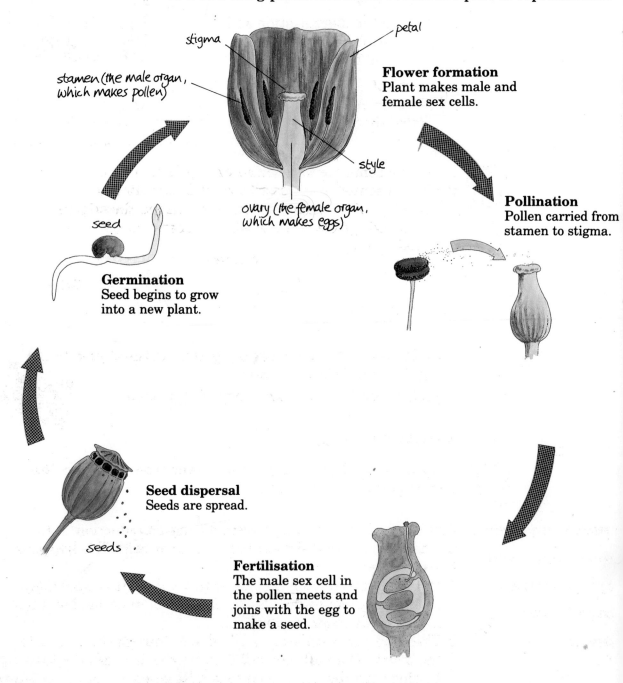

stigma

petal

stamen (the male organ, which makes pollen)

Flower formation
Plant makes male and female sex cells.

style

ovary (the female organ, which makes eggs)

Pollination
Pollen carried from stamen to stigma.

seed

Germination
Seed begins to grow into a new plant.

Seed dispersal
Seeds are spread.

seeds

Fertilisation
The male sex cell in the pollen meets and joins with the egg to make a seed.

Collect a summary of this diagram and complete it. Stick it into your book.

1 Gently pull the flower apart using the tweezers.

2 Find • a petal
• a stamen (the male part)
• the stigma, style and ovary (the female parts)

3 Stick these parts of the flower into your book and label them.

1 Write a sentence to describe what pollination is.
2 Write a sentence to describe what fertilisation is.
3 During pollination the pollen gets stuck to the stigma. The drawings below show what happens next.

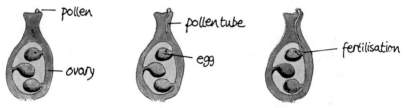

Describe how the male sex cell gets from the stigma to the egg. Use the following words:

pollen pollen tube ovary egg fertilisation

B Main events

Copy the following passage. Put the words on the left in the correct place in the passage.

insects fertilisation

male style wind

egg pollination

stigma tube

female

Flowering plants have a problem during reproduction. How can the _____ sex cell meet the _____ sex cell? This happens in two stages.

1 Pollen is moved from one flower to another. It is carried by _____ or blown in the _____. The pollen must land on the _____. This stage is called _____.

2 The pollen grows a long _____ down through the _____ to the ovary. The male sex cell then travels through the tube. It joins with the _____. This stage is called _____.

Problem

Site the seed

Your problem is to advise a government about the best place to plant a new food crop.
Here is a sketch map of the country.

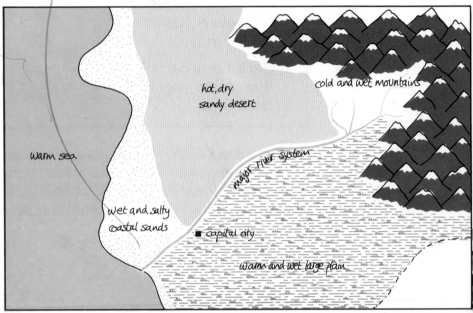

You know that seed germinates in a few days. You have to find out how well the plant will grow in the
- sandy desert
- large plain
- mountains
- coastal sands.

Collect

Packet of seeds
Anything else you need

Design some experiments to solve the problem.
Hints
- The seed will germinate on wet paper.

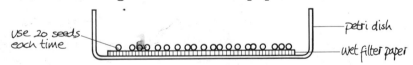

- You will have to do several different experiments.
- You will have to make sure that any test you do is **fair**.

Now solve the problem

Write a short report for the government. Include a description of your experiment(s) and your results. Give advice about the best place to plant the crop.

Letters page

These letters are about imaginary science problems. Discuss the letters with your partner. Decide how to answer each letter (kindly).

Dear Uncle Harvey,

I can't seem to get pollinated. My friends all say I'm not bad looking but no insect will come near me. Can you give me any advice. I enclose a recent photo.

Yours,
Paula N.

Dear Uncle Harvey

All the men on T.v. have hairy chests. I don't even have any under my arms. Am I normal I am 9 years old

Fluff

Dear Harvey

Why is it that salmon like myself have to make so many eggs? Chickens only make a few, humans make even less. No wonder they have time to go fishing! Please explain why life is so unfair to fish

your friend,

Small Fry

Dear Uncle Harvey

This is my photo. You can see that I am not smiling. I live in a pond that is full of wonderful, beautiful frogs. They all have so much fun and they mate every spring. I am missing out. What is wrong with me? Tad Pole

Konrad Lorenz

Konrad Lorenz was born in Austria in 1903. As a small boy he kept a houseful of all sorts of pets. This love of animals influenced his life's work. He trained as a doctor, but he became interested in how animals behave. Some scientists study animals in the laboratory but Lorenz preferred to observe them outside in their natural surroundings.

Some of his most important work was done with wild geese. He collected and hatched eggs from wild geese. The newly hatched goslings thought that he was their mummy! They followed Lorenz everywhere. If he went shopping in the village then they trailed after him in a line. If he went swimming then they did too. The other villagers were very amused. Lorenz realised that following their mother helped the goslings to survive in the wild. He called the behaviour **imprinting**.

Lorenz went on to study more complicated animal behaviour. He wrote a lot about courtship behaviour in birds. He explained why courtship always came before mating. He also studied aggression.

Lorenz worked with wild animals but some of his ideas have helped other scientists to understand human behaviour. Konrad Lorenz was awarded a Nobel Prize in 1973.

1 Copy and complete the personal history file about Konrad Lorenz.

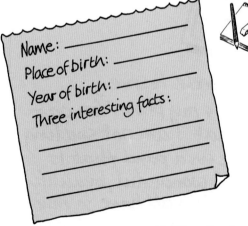

Name: _____
Place of birth: _____
Year of birth: _____
Three interesting facts:
_____
_____
_____

2 Use the books in the classroom or books from a library to find out more about Lorenz and his work. Write a paragraph about what you find out. The key words to look up in the index are **Lorenz**, **imprinting**, **instinct**, **courtship behaviour**, **aggression**.

Extensions

Going round in circles

1 Cut three circles of card.
2 Put a short line of colour on the card as shown below.

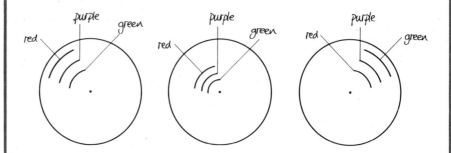

3 Stick one card onto the motor with Blu-Tack. Turn the motor on and spin the card.

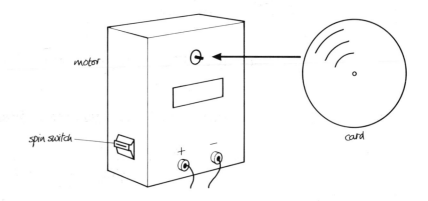

4 Look closely at the pattern on the spinning card. Repeat with another card.
5 Stick the cards into your book.

1 Draw what you saw on each spinning card. Use the coloured pencils.
2 Which card produced the best effect?

Design your own spinning card if you have time.

Salt, vinegar and (marble) chips

Collect

Bottle of salt
Bottle of marble chips
Bottle of vinegar
Test-tube rack
2 test tubes
Safety glasses

Find out what happens when you add vinegar to salt and when you add vinegar to marble chips.

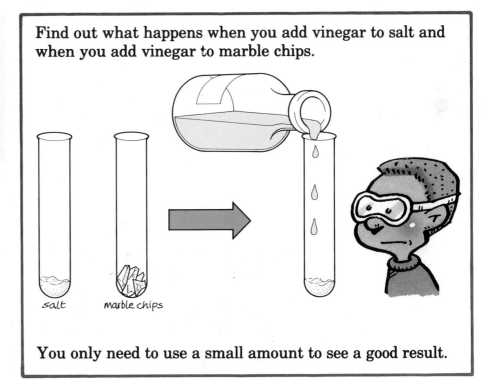

salt   marble chips

You only need to use a small amount to see a good result.

Write a short report about your experiment. You should include

Your own title

The method (what you did):

The result (what happened):

Filling time

You are going to practise some simple scientific skills that you will use often. There are three skills to practise. It is important to think about safety even when you do simple things.

Collect

Small beaker of water
Dropper
Dimple tile

1 Use the dropper to fill one of the dimples to the brim.
2 If you spill any water or overfill the dimple, try again.

Collect

Sample tube
Black paper
Spatula
Bottle of salt.

1 The sample tube has a mark on it. Put the sample tube on the black paper.
2 Use the spatula to fill the sample tube up to the mark with salt. If you spill any salt on the black paper start again.

Collect

Test tube
Test-tube rack
Spatula
Dropper
Bottle of acid
Bottle of green powder
Safety glasses

1 The test tube has two marks on it. Fill it to the first mark with the green powder. Use your new skill.
2 Fill it to the second mark with acid. Use your new skill.
3 Mix the powder and acid. Gently shake the tube from side to side. Knock it against the first finger of your other hand.
4 Watch (and feel) what happens.

1 Why is it important to be good at the three skills you have practised? Write down one safety reason for each.
2 Why should you never mix chemicals in a test tube by turning the test tube upside down with your thumb on the top?
3 Write down as much as you can about what happened in the final experiment.

Animal bits

Leroy is exploring an unusual planet called **Yonneb**. He is very interested in animals, but he needs your help to make a scientific study. He has sent you the following report about the two largest animals on Yonneb, the **plookle** and the **trockle**.

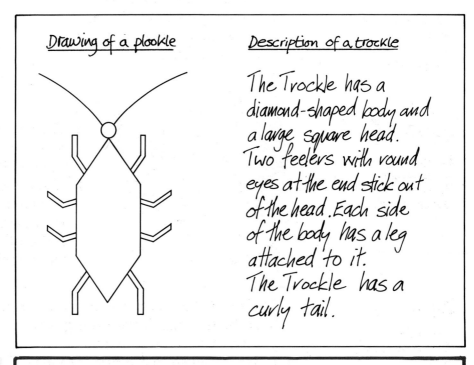

Drawing of a plookle

Description of a trockle

The Trockle has a diamond-shaped body and a large square head. Two feelers with round eyes at the end stick out of the head. Each side of the body has a leg attached to it. The Trockle has a curly tail.

Collect

Box of animal bits

Use the bits from the box to build a model of
- a plookle
- a trockle.

1 Draw a picture of a trockle.
2 Describe the plookle.
3 Leroy has sent you two animals, known as Spess and Imen. Using the pictures below, decide whether Spess and Imen are trockles or plookles.

Spess

Imen

Signs of life

When the American Mariner probe landed on Mars it was able to test the Martian soil for living things. Unfortunately the experiments could not give very definite results and there was no astronaut present to carry out more detailed observations.

Imagine that you are Chuck L. Peyton Jnr, Astronaut 1st class. You have leapt down from the first manned Mars probe and just narrowly avoided stepping on a small squelchy thing.

1 Describe five simple observations that you could quickly make to indicate if the squelchy thing was a living thing.
2 Describe one longer test that you could do to indicate whether the squelchy thing is alive. (Don't do anything that will kill it!)

An eye for the plants

Look closely at the three pairs of plants below.

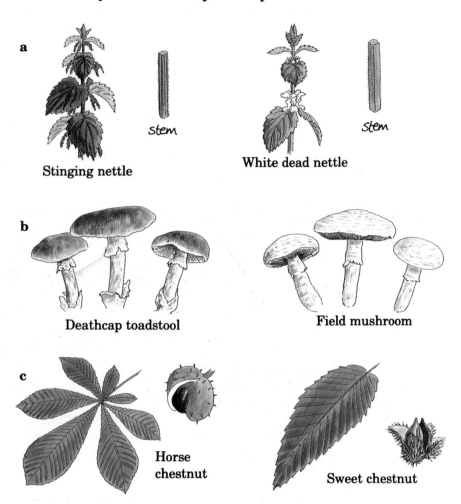

a

Stinging nettle   stem   White dead nettle   stem

b

Deathcap toadstool   Field mushroom

c

Horse chestnut   Sweet chestnut

What **two** important details allow you to tell the difference
between the two types of **a** nettles?
                    b mushrooms?
                    c chestnuts?

Plant sets

Plants are divided into sets by identifying important details.

The important details are **flowers** and **seeds**. Plants can be divided into two sets, **flowering** (seed-carrying) plants and **non-flowering** (seedless) plants.

These are flowering plants   These are non-flowering plants

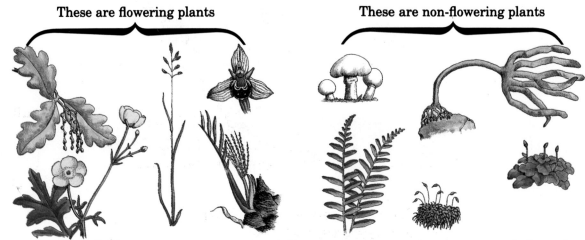

1 **a** What is the difference between the two sets of plants?
  b Why is it sometimes difficult to spot this important detail?
2 Look at the plant sets below.
  a Which set contains four flowering plants?
  b Which set contains four non-flowering plants?
  c Which plant is the odd one out in each set?

Set A

Set B

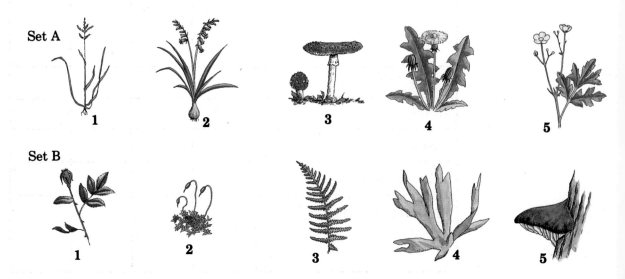

Leaf it out

Collect

Sheet of paper
Soft pencil
or wax crayon

1 Visit some local trees.
2 Collect a leaf from four different types of tree.
3 Make a bark rubbing of the four trees.

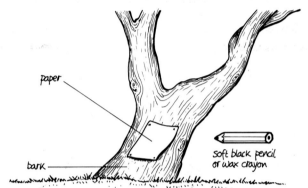

paper

bark

soft black pencil
or wax crayon

Rub your pencil
over the paper

4 Stick each leaf into your book.
   Number each leaf.

Copy and complete this table.

	Leaf 1	Leaf 2	Leaf 3	Leaf 4
Shape (draw)				
Length (measure)				
Width (measure)				
Colour				
Habitat of tree				
Bark rubbing from tree				

Unusual mammals

You are going to brighten up your science laboratory. Your work will go on the wall for all to see and admire.

1 Find out about **one** unusual mammal. Use the school library, local library or the books available in the classroom.

2 Draw a poster which includes
   a a sketch of your chosen mammal.
   b a few facts which show that it is an unusual mammal.

Hints
Use the index and contents pages of the books.
Skim and scan any useful pages.

Some picture clues

Making keys

You can begin to make a key by dividing the objects into two sets. One set will be different from the other in **one** important detail. These sets are then divided again and again until each object is in a set on its own.

For example, look at these pets.

Dog

Manx cat

Rabbit

Horse

1 Copy the table.
  If the pet has the detail then put a tick in that box.

	Dog	Cat	Rabbit	Horse
Short tail				
Long tail				
Short ears				
Long ears				

2 Copy the branching key into your book.
  Use the information from your table to complete the key.

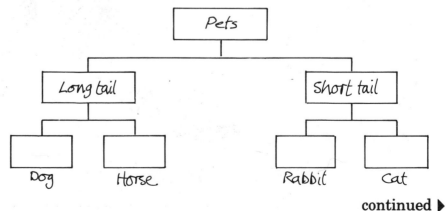

continued ▶

3 Look at the pictures of rock-pool fish.
Use the following clues to make a branching key.

Rockpool fish

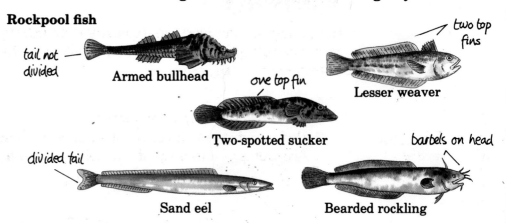

tail not divided — Armed bullhead

two top fins — Lesser weaver

one top fin — Two-spotted sucker

divided tail — Sand eel

barbels on head — Bearded rockling

4 Look at the pictures of garden birds.
Make a branching key.

Garden birds

Blue tit

Robin

Chaffinch

Starling

Blackbird

House sparrow

5 Your teacher may allow you to make a class key. Here are some important details to look out for.

freckles

tongue rolling

left/right handed

cross hands

sex

hair type

SPA2

Fairly dry

Some liquids evaporate more easily than others. If you want to compare liquids then you must make sure that your experiment is fair.

Collect

Piece of filter paper
Two droppers
Bottle of alcohol
Timer
Scissors

1 Cut the filter paper into quarters.
2 Put one drop of water on one quarter. Using the other dropper put one drop of alcohol on another quarter.

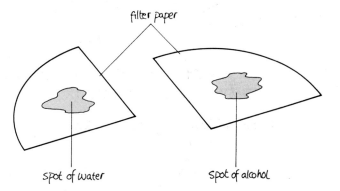

3 Time how long it takes for each drop to dry up.
4 Now do the following and time how long it takes for each drop to dry up.

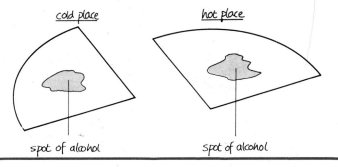

1 Write a report about this experiment. Include the method (a description of what you did), a drawing and a note of your results.

2 What did you do to make the experiment fair?

Vanishing varnish

Water is not the only solvent. Other liquids can also dissolve substances.

CARE
Many solvents are **harmful**.
Some solvents are
flammable.

Harmful

Flammable

Collect

Slide with 5 streaks
of nail varnish
Cotton wool
Tweezers
5 solvents (water,
propanone, alcohol,
turpentine, ethyl
ethanoate)
Safety glasses

1 Put the slide on a heatproof mat. Make sure that there are no flames in the laboratory.

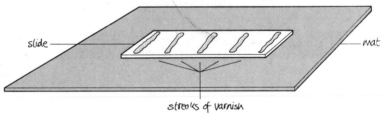

2 Put about five drops of one of the solvents on a small piece of cotton wool.
3 Pick up the cotton wool with tweezers.
4 Rub **one** of the streaks of nail varnish with the cotton wool.
5 Count how many rubs are needed to remove the streak.

6 Repeat with the other solvents.

1 Describe the method (what you did).
2 Make a table for your results.
3 Which solvent(s) would make good nail-varnish remover?

Be a rock star

There are several different types of rocks.
- **Igneous** rocks have formed quickly as molten rock has cooled down. They are made of small crystals and are hard.
- **Sedimentary** rocks have formed in layers. They have few crystals and they are usually quite soft.
- **Metamorphic** rocks have formed slowly when other rocks have been heated and pushed together. They have crystals, sometimes large ones, and they are very hard.

Igneous (basalt)   Sedimentary (sandstone)   Metamorphic (hornfels)

Collect

Samples of named rock
Hand lens (or binocular microscope)
Nail
Geological hammer (if available)
Safety glasses

Using your equipment find out what rock type each of the rock samples is.
You will need to test for
- hardness
- presence of crystals
- size of crystals.

 Complete a report sheet like the following one.

Name	Hard	Any Crystals	Size of crystal	Type of rock
Flintstone	✓	✓	5mm	?

119

TLC

TLC means **thin-layer chromatography**. It is a way of separating mixtures without using paper. It is very accurate and it works with very small amounts of mixture.

1 Put an ink spot on the white powder as shown.

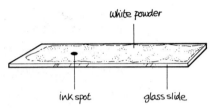

white powder

ink spot   glass slide

2 Stand the slide in alcohol.

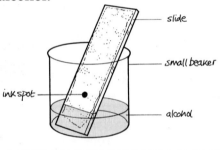

slide

small beaker

ink spot

alcohol

1 Draw a diagram to show what you did.
2 Draw the results of your experiment in colour.
3 What are the differences between TLC and the paper chromatography that you tried earlier?

Orange perfume

The separating technique of **distillation** is used in the perfume industry. Many plants contain smelly oils which can be put into perfume. The oil is taken out by heating the plant material and distilling the vapour.

Collect

Fresh orange peel
Wire gauze basket
Thread
Bunsen burner and mat
Tripod stand
2 flasks
Condenser
Safety glasses
Ice
Clamp stand

1 Quarter fill one flask with water.
2 Put the orange peel in the wire basket. Hang it above the water level with thread.
3 Finish setting up the apparatus as shown below.

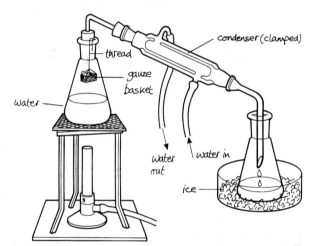

4 Heat the water **gently** to produce steam. The steam will take the oil out of the orange peel. Collect the oil for about two minutes. It should smell tremendously nice!

Write a full report about this experiment.
Include
- the title
- the method (description of what you did)
- a diagram
- and a spot of perfumed oil in your book

Energy in store

There are three different types of stored energy: potential energy, nuclear energy and chemical energy.

Potential energy is the type of energy that a stone has at the top of a hill and . . .

Chemical energy is the type of energy that food has and . . .

Nuclear energy is the type of energy used in atomic explosions and . . .

1 Write down three types of stored energy.
2 Copy and complete the table.

Types of stored energy	Two examples	
	a	b
	a	b
	a	b

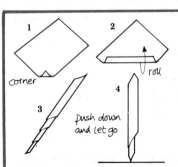

corner

roll

push down and let go

A piece of paper can be rolled diagonally to make a spring. This spring can store energy.

Use different sizes of the same kind of paper (half a sheet, quarter and so on) and find out
a if a small spring stores more energy than a large spring.
b if a loose coil stores more energy than a tight coil.

Difficult energy changes

Sometimes it is difficult to identify an energy change when something happens. This can be because

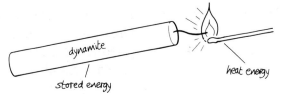

- you start with more than one form of energy

- one of the forms is difficult to spot

- the starting form of energy changes into another form and this form then changes again

- many different energy changes happen at once.

Do the following experiments.

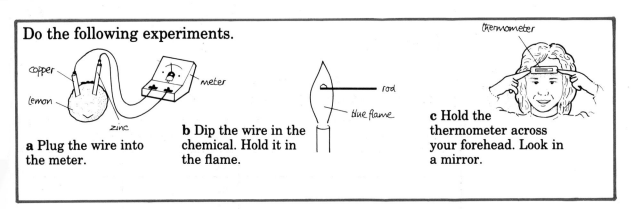

a Plug the wire into the meter.

b Dip the wire in the chemical. Hold it in the flame.

c Hold the thermometer across your forehead. Look in a mirror.

1 Write a report about **one** of your experiments. Your report should be like the description of the bunsen burner on page 56. Include **all** the energy changes.

2 Identify the most important energy change in

a growing plant

b moving helicopter

c film in a camera

d lighted candle

Machines that go on forever

A machine changes one form of energy into another form. However, all machines waste some of the energy that they start with.

A car changes stored energy into movement energy. Yet a lot of the stored energy from the fuel is wasted. It is lost mainly as unused heat energy and some sound energy.

Go to one of the machines in the room and make it work.

1 Write a report about one of the machines. Write down **all** the energy changes in the machine.
2 Explain why this machine eventually stops.
3 Look at the machine in the picture.

Is energy wasted in this machine or can it go on forever?

Food chains

Food contains stored energy. Animals eat to obtain this
energy. An animal which eats plants is called a **herbivore**.
An animal which eats other animals is called a **carnivore**.
An animal which eats both plants and animals is called an
omnivore.

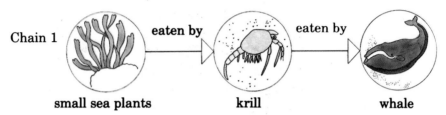

Chain 1

small sea plants   krill   whale

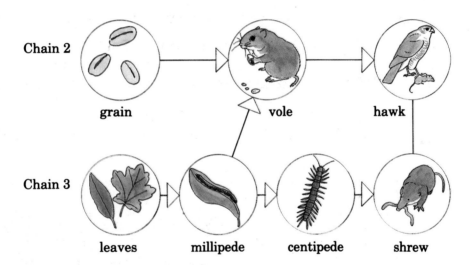

Chain 2

grain   vole   hawk

Chain 3

leaves   millipede   centipede   shrew

---

1 Copy the above food chains into your book (words only).
2 Put a green circle round each herbivore.
   Put a red circle round each carnivore.
   Put a yellow circle round each omnivore.

---

1 What is a food chain?
2 Give the meaning of the words omnivore, herbivore and
carnivore.
3 Would you rather be a herbivore, a carnivore or an
omnivore? Give reasons for your answer.
4 What is the real starting point of all the food chains? (*Hint*:
where do green plants get their energy from?)

More measurement puzzles

Solve the following puzzles.
For each puzzle you should
- record each measurement.
- write a sentence to explain how you solved each puzzle.

How do you measure. . . ?

a the mass of one paper clip

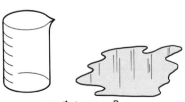

mass A + mass B

b the mass of 50 cm³ of water

c the volume of one drop of water

water + stone = ?

d the volume of a stone

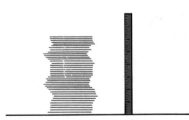

e the thickness of one sheet of paper

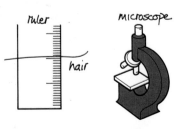

f the thickness of one hair

Zooming around

You can find out how fast objects are travelling by measuring the time taken to travel a known distance. Two measurements are needed to calculate the speed.

$$\text{speed} = \frac{\text{distance}}{\text{time}}$$

100 METRE DASH
PREVIOUS RECORD 5 HOURS 32 MINS
FINISH
START

Collect

Clipboard
Paper and pencil
Timer
Two markers
Tape measure

1 Your teacher will tell you where to do this experiment. Work with a partner.
2 Measure 100 m using the tape. Mark the beginning and the end.
3 Record how long it takes for you to
   a walk 100 m
   b jog 100 m
   c run 100 m.

Copy and complete the table below.

Pace	Distance	Time taken to cover 100 m.	Calculated speed in metres per second
walk	100 m		

Cool it

In an experiment a scientist often measures **change**. For example, the colour of a liquid may change or the mass of a solid may change.

A scientist records the changing measurement over a period of time. Often the results can be shown in a line graph. Temperature is one measurement which often changes over time.

Collect

Thermometer
Elastic band
Sheet of graph paper
Piece of cotton wool
Bottle of propanone
Clock
Watch or timer

1 Wrap the cotton wool carefully around the bulb of the thermometer. Hold it in place with the elastic band.

 *make sure you can see the start of the scale.*

2 Copy the table below into your book.

	Time					
	Start	2 min	4 min	6 min	8 min	10 min
Temperature						

3 Add ten drops of propanone to the cotton wool. The propanone will evaporate and cool the cotton wool. Look at the clock. Read and record the temperature.
4 Record the temperature every two minutes until the table is complete.

Draw a line graph of your results. Use the hints below to help you.

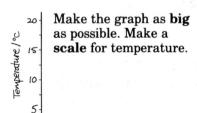 Make the graph as **big** as possible. Make a **scale** for temperature.

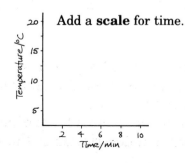 Add a **scale** for time.

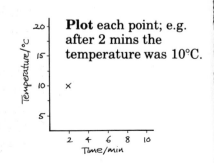 **Plot** each point; e.g. after 2 mins the temperature was 10°C.

Batteries

A battery contains chemicals which store energy. When you use a battery the stored energy becomes electrical energy. The energy change is

stored → electrical

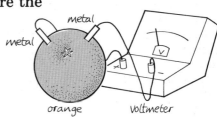

symbol for a voltmeter

1 Wash a 5p coin and a 2p coin. Join the coins with a wire. Hold them apart on your tongue.

2 **Collect** a voltmeter and two wires. Each wire is attached to a piece of metal. Stick the pieces of metal into the orange. Note the reading on the voltmeter.
(A voltmeter can measure the strength of a battery.)

metal

metal

orange

voltmeter

3 **Collect** a set of metals and a beaker of vinegar. Make this model battery.

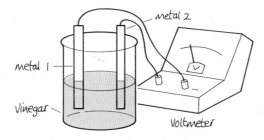

metal 2

metal 1

vinegar

voltmeter

Find out which pair of metals gives the highest reading on the voltmeter.

1 Describe what happened in experiment **1**.
2 Draw the diagram for experiment **2**. What was the voltmeter reading?
3 Write a report about experiment **3**. Include a diagram, a description of the method and the result.

Continuity tester

An electric current cannot usually flow across a gap in a circuit. For example, these gaps stop the current.

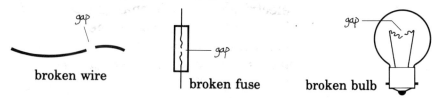

broken wire   broken fuse   broken bulb

An electrician uses a **continuity tester** to find a gap in a broken circuit. The damage is repaired by closing the gap.

This is a continuity tester.

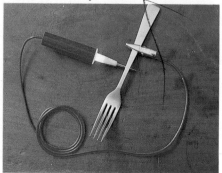

It contains this circuit.

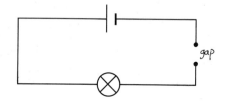

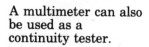

A multimeter can also be used as a continuity tester.

---

1 **Collect** a set of test wires, and the items needed to build the circuit shown above. Use it to find out which wires are broken.

2 **Collect** a multimeter and a set of electrical components. Your teacher will show you how to use the multimeter. Use the multimeter to check
 a the broken wires from your first experiment
 b the electrical components for gaps.

---

1 Draw a circuit diagram of a continuity tester.
2 Describe how you used a continuity tester to find a broken wire.
3 The multimeter was set to measure resistance.
 a What reading do you get when there is a gap in the circuit.
 b What is the meaning of **resistance**? (Look at page 80)
 c Does an air gap have a high or a low resistance to current?

Hot wires

When a wire resists electric
current it heats up. Some
electrical energy is changed
into heat energy. Sometimes
the wire gets so hot that it
glows. This effect is used in
the design of
  • heaters
  • fuses.

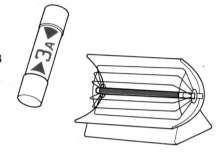

Collect

Piece of resistance
wire
Piece of fuse wire
Heatproof mat
Power supply
Connecting wires
with crocodile clips
Safety glasses

1 Make each wire into a coil by wrapping it around a
  pencil. Take out the pencil.

2 Set up this circuit using the resistance wire first.

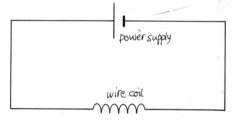

3 Turn the power supply to 2 volts. Switch on. Turn the
  voltage to 4 volts then to 6 volts.
4 Observe the wire for 10 seconds then switch off.
5 Now use the fuse wire instead of the resistance wire.

1 Draw the circuit.
2 a What happens to the resistance wire when you
     increase the voltage?
  b How could this be used in the home to make a
     heater?
3 a What happens to the fuse wire when you increase
     the voltage?
  b How could this be used in the home to make circuits
     safer?

Upstairs/downstairs

If there are stairs in your house then you need two switches
to control the stair light—one upstairs and one downstairs.
This design problem can be solved by using 2 two-way
switches.

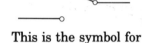

This is the symbol for
a two-way switch

Collect

Bulb
2 batteries
6 wires
2 two-way switches

Try to design and build a circuit which will switch one
light on and off from two different switches.

Use the two-way switches like this.

Solve the design problem. When the circuit is working
show it to your teacher.

1 Draw a circuit diagram of your circuit.
2 Explain how your circuit works.

Measuring electricity

The amount of electricity flowing in a circuit is called the **current**. Current is measured in **amperes (A)**.

This ammeter is showing a current of 0.2 A.

The battery gives the current a steady push. The strength of the push is called **voltage**. Voltage is measured in **volts (V)**.

This voltmeter is showing a voltage of 1.5 V.

Collect

Ammeter
Voltmeter
Bulb
9 wires
4 batteries
Graph paper

1 Set up this circuit.

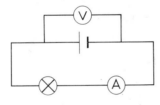

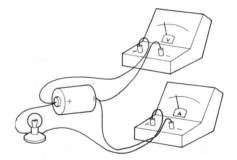

Note • Connect the **black** terminal of the ammeter to the **negative** (−) end of the battery and the other terminal to the bulb.
• Connect the **black** terminal of the voltmeter to the **negative** (−) end of the battery and the other voltmeter terminal to the positive end.

2 Find out what happens to the voltage and the current when you increase the number of batteries in the circuit.

1 Draw the circuit diagram.
2 Make a table to record the number of batteries, voltage and current.
3 Draw a line graph of current against voltage.
4 Describe what the graph shows.

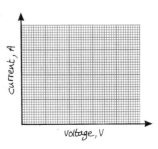

Live electricity

Many living things use electricity. Here are some examples.

1 Some fish can generate electricity in their bodies to find their way about in murky water. Special muscles send out small electrical signals which are used for navigation.

2 There is a lot of electrical activity in animal brains including your own. This EEG (electroencephalograph) traces the electrical activity in a human brain.

 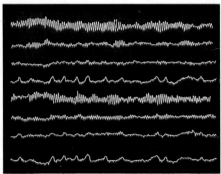

3 There is also electrical activity in the heart. When the heart muscle contracts the heartbeat is accompanied by electrical changes. We can measure these using an ECG (electrocardiogram). This is a trace from an ECG.

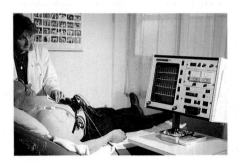 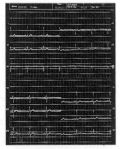

continued ▶

4 Electricity can be used to repair faults in the body.

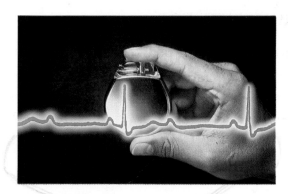

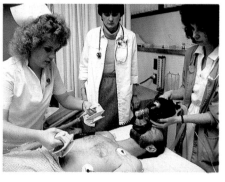

A faulty heart can be controlled by an artificial pacemaker which uses electricity to make the heart beat at the correct rate.

A heart which stops can be restarted by giving it an electric shock.
The cardiac arrest team must stand back from the patient while a large voltage is applied to the chest.

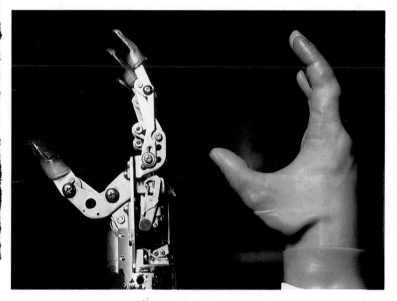

An artificial limb can be controlled by a little electric motor. The motor is switched on and off by muscle contractions in the limb stump.

1 Write a short paragraph about electricity in living creatures.
2 Write a short paragraph about the use of electricity in medicine.

Flea in your eye

This is an outline of the body shape of a water flea (called *Daphnia*).

A water flea is tiny and you need a microscope to see the important body parts. The following parts are missing from the drawing above: legs, antennae, heart, eye and long gut tube.

Collect

Water flea
Slide

1 Copy the outline of the water flea.
2 Put a water flea on a slide. Make sure the animal is in a drop of water.

3 Focus the microscope on the water flea. Find the
   • legs
   • heart
   • eyes
   • long gut tube
   • antennae
4 Add the important body parts to your outline shape. Label them.
5 Return the water flea to its container.
6 Have a look for other animals in the pondwater that is available. Draw any animal or plant that you see.

Living cells

All living cells make a chemical that causes bubbles in hydrogen peroxide solution. The bubbles show clearly at low magnification with a hand lens. So hydrogen peroxide can be used to test for **living** cells.

Test each sample as follows:

1 Make a slide of the substance.

2 Add **one drop** of hydrogen peroxide solution. Cover with a cover slip.

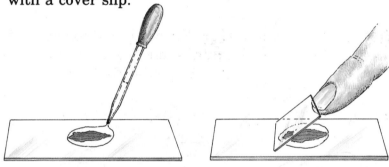

3 Focus the hand lens on the slide and look for bubbles. Are the cells alive?

 Write a report about your experiment. Put your results in a table.

Messages in cells

The plan for your body is inside the nucleus of each of your cells. People look different mainly because their plans are different.

The plan is in the form of a chemical code. The code is carried by a chemical called **DNA**.

The code is made up of small bits called **genes**, rather like this sentence is made up of bits called words. Each gene contains one part of the plan for your body. There are genes for hair colour, blood group and so on.

A single strand of DNA is called a **chromosome** and it contains thousands of genes. When cells are dividing you can sometimes see the chromosomes using a microscope.

The chromosomes are all jumbled up in the cell. However we draw them like this.

A human female has this set of chromosomes

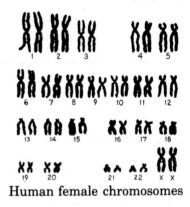

Human female chromosomes

1 Why do people look different?
2 What is a chromosome?
3 How many chromosomes are in the human female chromosome set?
4 Look at this picture of the human male chromosome set. How is it different from the female chromosome set?

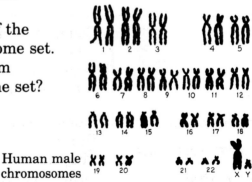

Human male chromosomes

5 What information do you think is on the Y chromosome?

How humans reproduce

The table shows some important events in the life of a person. All these events are linked to sexual reproduction.

	Important event	What happens
Maturity		The person makes either female or male sex cells. Only now is the person able to reproduce. He or she has reached sexual maturity.
Courtship and mating		The woman and man meet and get to know each other. If they mate then sperm are passed into the body of the woman.
Fertilisation	egg cell / sperm	The sperm swim towards the egg. One sperm enters the egg to fertilise it.
Embryo growth	6 weeks / 8 weeks	The fertilised egg divides again and again to form a ball of cells. This embryo keeps on growing and develops into a baby.
Birth		The baby is born. In humans the baby comes from the mother's body. The baby begins to breathe and to take food.
Growth	baby / child / adult	The baby gets bigger and grows into a mature adult.

1 Collect a summary of this table and complete it. Stick it into your book.
2 Copy the following passage. Put the words on the left in the correct place in this passage.

sperm   inside

embryo   reproduce

egg   mating

fertilisation   adult

Human fertilisation occurs _____ the woman's body. During _____ the sperm are squirted into the woman. They swim to meet the _____. One _____ enters it and forms an embryo. This is called _____. The _____ then grows in the woman's body. After about nine months a baby is born. It eventually reaches maturity and becomes an _____. The person is now able to _____.

Seed dispersal

After fertilisation the ovary wall becomes a fruit. The ovules inside the ovary become seeds. Seeds have to be spread away from the parent plant to give them a better chance to grow well. Plants disperse their seeds in different ways.

Blown in the wind	Eaten or partly eaten	Carried on an animal	Thrown by explosion

parachute of hairs

Dandelion

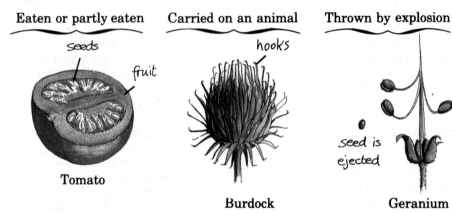

seeds

fruit

Tomato

hooks

Burdock

seed is ejected

Geranium

1 Look at the pictures above. What important details help these seeds to be dispersed.?
2 Here is a picture of a seed and fruit collection. How would each of the seeds be dispersed?

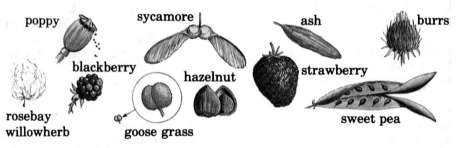

poppy

sycamore

ash

burrs

blackberry

hazelnut

strawberry

rosebay willowherb

goose grass

sweet pea

3 Copy and complete this table.

	Blown in the wind	Carried on animal	Eaten or partly eaten	Thrown by explosion
Common features				
Four examples				

Index

Acknowledgements

CARTOONS: Ainslie MacLeod/Domino Studios
LINE DRAWINGS: Ian Foulis Associates
NATURAL HISTORY DIAGRAMS: David Webb/ Linden Artists
COVER PHOTO: Rob Matheson/Zefa

The following have provided photographs or given permission for photographs to be reproduced:

p. 13   *all photos* Tom Harrison

p. 19   *top right* Barnaby's Picture Library; *bottom left* European Space Agency; *bottom right* Klaus Hackenberg/ZEFA

p. 20   BBC Hulton Picture Library

p. 37   *top right* NASA/Woodmansterne; *bottom left* Photri/ZEFA

p. 38   BBC Hulton Picture Library

p. 45   *top left* Soames Summerhays/Biofotos; *top right and bottom left* GSF Picture Library; *bottom right* Robert Jureit/Planet Earth

p. 51   Desert – *left and top right GSF Picture Library; bottom right* Barnaby's Picture Library. Hot springs – GSF Picture Library. Deep sea – *all photos* Peter David/Planet Earth Pictures. Antarctic ice – *top left* J.W.H. Conroy/Biofotos; *top right* P. V. Tearle/Planet Earth Pictures; *bottom left* K.J. Gilbert/ Barnaby's Picture Library; *bottom right* Bryn Campbell/Biofotos

p. 52   BBC Hulton Picture Library

p. 59   *far left* European Space Agency; *centre left* Hubrich/ZEFA; *centre right* NASA/Science Photo Library; *far right* Tom McHugh/ Science Photo Library

p. 60   ZEFA

p. 62   Discovery of electricity – *left* Electricty Council Archives; *right* Institution of Electrical Engineers. Making eletricity – *top* Central Electricity Generating Board; *bottom left* ZEFA; *bottom right* Theojac/ZEFA. Working with electricity – *all photos* Electricity Council. Using electricity sensibly – *all photos* Eleticity Council

p. 64   BBC Hulton Picture Library

p. 68   *left* Mansell Collection; *right* Melvin Prueitt, Los Alamos National Laboratory/Science Photo Library

p. 74   Mansell Collection

p. 89   *top left* Electricity Council; *centre left and top right* ZEFA; *bottom left* Bramaz/ZEFA; *bottom right* British Rail Southern Region

p. 90   BBC Hulton Picture Library

p. 92   *top far left* David Leah/Science Photo Library; *top centre left* Martin Dohrn/Science Photo Library; *top centre right* Picture Point, London; *top far right* Dr Jeremy Burgess/ Science Photo Library; *bottom* Philip Harris

p. 97   Francis Leroy, Biocosmos/Science Photo Library

p. 104   Mary Evans Picture Library

p. 119   *left and right* GSF Picture Library; *centre* Astrid & Hans – Frieder Michler/Science Photo Library

p. 121   Boots

p. 122   *top left* Barnaby's Picture Library; *top centre* Ever Ready; *top right* Crown copyright; *bottom left* Steenmans/ZEFA; *bottom centre* Camping Gaz; *bottom right* Central Electricity Generating Board

p. 124   © 1989 M.C. Escher Heirs/Cordon Art, Baarn, Holland

p. 130   *left* Megger Instruments; *right David Purdie*

p. 134   *top left* Paulo Oliveira/Planet Earth Pictures; *top right* Ken Lucas/Planet Earth Pictures; *centre left* Alexander Tsiaras/Science Photo Library; *centre right* Jean Kennedy, Royal Free/Science Photo Library; *bottom left and right* Science Photo Library

p. 135   *top left* Bill Longcore/Science Photo Library; *top right* Grapes, Michaud/Science Photo Library; *bottom left* Claude Charlier/Science Photo Library; *bottom right* Limb Fitting Centre, Roehampton

p. 138   ZEFA